A
REASONED
FAITH

God
speaks
to an
atheistic
scientist

Thanks

I must first give thanks to Andy Duggan who boldly and lovingly shared his faith with me at work. He was the catalyst for the thirty-year faith journey that I describe in my book.

I am also grateful to the many pastors and prayer partners who have encouraged me along the way, too many to name individually. You have shaped my understanding of the Bible and helped me to mature in my faith. You have been there in the joyous times and throughout the many challenges of life. Thank you.

Thank you, Matt Bird and PublishU, for giving me the motivation and discipline to actually put pen to paper and turn the pipedream of a book into a reality. Thank you also to Mark, Christian, Paddy, Dennis and Clare, who spent time reading the first draft and providing such valuable critique. I hope that I have done you justice.

Lastly, thank you, Clare, for being such a godly wife and mother. You have been such an example to Amy, Izzy and Eliza and have modelled compassionate and sacrificial love to so many people throughout our marriage. This book is based on our shared faith journey and I am so glad that God placed you at my side to experience all we have together.

To those that I love who do not yet know Jesus, I pray that you will enjoy and be challenged by my story.

Contents

Introduction

I am writing this book for my family and friends and for future grandchildren. If others read it and are blessed by it, then even better. It is about a topic that some say today is, at best, irrelevant and, at worst, something that causes strife and division: specifically the Christian faith and how my worldview was changed in May 1991 when I became a Christian. I want to describe how I have been transformed in how I think and behave because of my relationship with Jesus. I want you, the reader, to understand that far from being irrelevant, we are talking about something, or should I say Someone, who can enrich your life right now and who determines what happens to you after you die.

I used to be an atheist and didn't believe in any form of God. I wrote a thesis on evolution as part of my Biology A-level and studied microbiology at university, which led to a career in the pharmaceutical industry. My consultancy business was in evidence-based medicine, looking at the data behind claims made by healthcare companies.

As a logical and mathematical person, I could not see how any sane person could believe in God. Instead, I thought science could explain everything.

I thought that Jesus was a fictional character, and the Bible was just a storybook. How could people put their faith in something that had absolutely no evidence to support it?

I thought that religion was something for other people, but not what I needed. It was for people who needed some kind of crutch.

I would argue that throughout history, religions have caused wars and various atrocities, such as burning people to death and blowing people up.

I would also argue that if there was a God, why is there poverty and disease in the world? Surely, a loving God would not allow innocent babies to die of horrible diseases or starve to death.

I thought that religion was about a moral code of conduct, and it didn't matter which religion you chose to follow; what counted was being good.

I was scared of death and liked the idea of a Heaven. I thought of myself as a good person because I hadn't murdered anyone, valued honesty and didn't lie or steal. Occasionally, I would help other people out and give to charity. A loving God would certainly take me into Heaven and reserve Hell for people like Hitler. I thought that when I am dead, that's it. There is nothing, and death is simply the end for us all.

My impression of church was based on the few occasions I went to a carol service, wedding or funeral. To me, it was old buildings, hard pews, old-fashioned people and long, boring sermons that were irrelevant. Who would want to go every Sunday? I even had an impression that churchgoers were mostly hypocritical do-gooders who looked down on the rest of us "sinners".

I believed that we get out of life what we put into it. Our destiny is purely determined by our efforts. My driving motivation was to be successful, and my measure of success was being good at work and making lots of money.

On the positive side of my character, I was logical, scientific, musical, clever, articulate and friendly. I was someone who liked reading a lot and had an enquiring mind. Looking back, I can see now that I was also full of pride, an arrogant know-it-all who liked arguing with people just for the sake of winning the debate. I was a selfish and hard-hearted individual who lusted after things I didn't yet have. Although I didn't swear much, I was a blasphemer, regularly using the term "Jesus Christ" as what I thought of as a mild expletive.

I don't know why, but I was also interested in astrology and star signs, as many people today are. I believed that the month I was born in affected who I was as a person and who I would be compatible (or not) with. I read my horoscope, which told me what would happen to me that day or week.

My worldview was totally changed when I became a Christian over thirty years ago. In this book, I would firstly like to share my testimony. How and why did such an atheist do an about-turn and ask Jesus Christ into his life?

The rest of the book will take each of those worldviews shared in this introduction and show how I now see things so differently. It is an example of eyes that were once blind seeing afresh through the lens of God. It is an example of how a relationship with Jesus transforms how you live and think.

Interestingly, I had all these strong opinions, having never read the Bible, having rarely been to church, and having never really investigated the evidence or spoken to any Christians. I just dismissed the idea of God out of hand.

If what happens to us after death is determined by something we do (or don't do) in this life, then what you believe is of huge importance. It is literally an eternal life-or-death decision.

I hope that those I love will read my story and then decide that there is enough personal evidence to explore the Christian faith further. My greatest desire is that you will discover the wonders of a personal relationship with Jesus Christ for yourself; guidance, strength, comfort and peace now and the promise of a perfect eternity in the life to come.

What a wonderful thought that one day we might meet in Heaven after this earthly life has finished. I might even get to meet some of my descendants for the first time in Heaven. How amazing if this book plays a part in that grand reunion.

I hope that you enjoy my story.

Chapter 1
Meeting with God

"In their hearts, humans plan their course, but the Lord establishes their steps."

– Proverbs 16:9

I believe that God has always had a hand in my life. Even before I believed in Him. He blessed me with a loving family and an exotic first few years living in Nairobi, Kenya. When my family returned to England in 1971, we did not have much money, but my memories are happy ones growing up in Clacton, Essex. I was good at school and loved reading and learning. My form teacher in Year Seven was a gifted musician, and with Dad's help and Mr Hurren's inspiration, I threw myself into learning piano. It has remained a passion ever since. I loved the school musicals we put on each year and enjoyed growing up by the seaside. Early life was good.

At school, I hated "boring" subjects like Religious Education and History and preferred the Sciences and Maths. At A-level, I wrote a thesis on evolution, and this hardened my views that the universe was a cosmic accident and that man and apes evolved from a common ancestor. I could not see how any logical person could believe in a God.

I was the first in my family to have the privilege of going to university, studying microbiology at Leeds, where I met Lisa, my first serious girlfriend. She was a Christian and on a Sunday, I would drop her off at church in the evening and then go and get a curry. At this point, my heart and my mind were utterly closed to the idea of any kind of faith.

When I graduated, my first job was as a medical sales representative for Searle Pharmaceuticals, initially in Norfolk. After less than two years I was a bit bored and considered changing careers. My parents had friends in Africa who ran a safari lodge and I dreamed of going out there to become a ranger and tourist guide. The owners were due to visit the UK and I was going to meet with them.

However, God had other plans.

My boss asked me to attend a management assessment centre for potential future leaders in the business. One candidate had dropped off the course, and I was making up the numbers. Despite being only twenty-three years old, the management team at Searle thought I did well, and a few weeks later, I was asked to apply for one of three sales training manager roles that had become available. I had less than the required two years of experience but was given a leadership role working with ten sales representatives in the West of England. God's plan for me was not in Africa; it was to eventually lead me to High Wycombe, and Searle's Head Office.

During the early 1990s, the NHS underwent significant changes, and Searle asked their training managers to meet with a new breed of decision-makers to understand those changes. That led to the formation of a new sales team who were to discuss funding matters with these local NHS fundholders. In turn, that led to Searle recruiting a marketing person to support this new sales team and I was given the job: three promotions in three years and a salary that had tripled. God continued to bless me despite hearing my atheist views and seeing my stubborn heart. He waited patiently for the right moment and that came at Easter 1991.

I had gone home to be with my family in Clacton for the holidays, and on Easter Sunday, I was munching my way through an Easter egg when I suddenly had a thought. Easter is not about chocolate eggs and bunnies. I realise now that this was the Holy Spirit speaking into my mind. I asked my mum if we had a Bible in the house, and she found an old one I was given at my Christening twenty-six years before. That Easter week, I started reading the Bible at night, starting at the beginning in Genesis, having no idea where the Easter story was. I don't think I ever got to the New Testament, but this was the start of my faith journey. Initially, I read some amazing stories. The Bible is full of them.

On April Fool's Day, 1991, I started my new marketing job at Searle and rented a house in Aylesbury to begin my new life. I now recognise that God was going to place Christians in my path so that I could get to know Him.

I found myself in an office next door to Andy Duggan, a "born-again" Christian and evangelist. He was a big guy with a big heart, and everyone loved and respected him, even though he was often the butt of God-squad jokes. He exuded a quiet strength and inner peace that was very attractive. At sales conferences, where over a hundred sales reps would be revelling it up, Andy would host Bible and prayer nights over a hot chocolate. He would print invites and hand them out to people, knowing that most would ignore him but that one or two would respond. He was a great example of living your life as a Christian at work. Many people, even the jesters, would creep into his office for some Godly wisdom and prayer when life got tough.

Soon after I started working at head office, there was a works' barbeque, and Andy was drinking non-alcoholic beer. He was known to be teetotal. I asked him why he didn't drink, and his answer stunned me, "God told me to stop."

"What do you mean 'God told you to stop'?" I responded. That started a series of fascinating discussions with him over a period of months.

Andy had grown up in London and came from a working-class family. Soon after he got married, he had a "burning bush" moment with God who told him to change his ways. He was one of the few people I have met who have had such a significant encounter with God where it instantly changed him. Again, I now recognise the work of the Holy Spirit falling upon Andy and God speaking to him. This amazing spiritual encounter led Andy to invite Jesus into his life, and God used him as an evangelist from then on.

Andy's strength was his simplicity. He was an ordinary bloke leading an everyday life, and yet he spoke of a God who was absolutely real to him. He spoke of the need to be born again and transformed on the inside rather than just being religious. I didn't understand everything that he said, but I found myself enjoying these conversations with a man who seemed to have such wisdom despite a lack of formal education.

I asked my usual questions: Why does God allow suffering? Why do good people struggle and sometimes bad people get everything? What about dinosaurs and evolution? Deep down, I was afraid of death, and Andy had such a conviction of Heaven that it was attractive. I liked the idea of there being life after death. Always, Andy had a wise answer that struck home. God was beginning to speak through Andy to me by answering several questions with conviction.

Andy invited me to a Full Gospel Businessmen's Fellowship dinner at the Littlebury Hotel in Bicester one evening. It was attended by ordinary businessmen, which helped counter my view that Christians were a bit sad and a bit weird. Not a sandal in sight! We had an enjoyable meal, and the after-dinner speaker was a retired Bishop from Singapore. He was funny and engaging, and I enjoyed the talk. Afterwards, there was an offer to go for prayer and Andy joined the queue to ask for healing for his back. He came back with a smile on his face and suggested I also go forward. I did so as a kind of experiment. I thought, if there is a God, then maybe I will meet Him through prayer, and if there isn't, then nothing will happen.

I don't know why, but as I got near the front of the queue, I felt nervous, and my heart started hammering. When it was my turn, I simply said, "I'm not a Christian, but if you want to pray for me, then that's OK".

The wise old man with a lovely wrinkled-up face smiled at me and asked about my relationship with my Father. I responded that Dad and I were good friends as well as father and son. I have always had an excellent relationship with him.

He smiled again and told me that I also had a heavenly Father who loved me and wanted a relationship with me. He prophesied over me, saying that one day I would lead my earthly father to my Heavenly One. That would not happen for another twenty-five years, and it was amazing to hear that, given that I was still an atheist at this stage.

Then he held his hands over my head and prayed for the Holy Spirit to fill me. I had heard of God and Jesus but never really thought anything about the third member of the Trinity, the Holy Spirit.

I can only say that something dramatic happened to me when he prayed. I felt peace and love flood me from my head to my toes. All the cares of life seemed to get washed away. It was a tangible, physical and emotional feeling. I knew then that something big had happened to me when that man prayed. I felt it! Andy could see it too, when I returned to my seat.

When I drove home that night, I opened the new Bible that Andy had given me, and it was like God started speaking to me through the words I read.

"I am the light of the world and whoever follows Me will never walk in darkness" (John 8:12). What wonderful words. None of us want to walk in the dark.

"Simon, I will make you a fisher of men" (Matthew 4:19). I didn't even know that there was a Simon in the Bible (the Apostle Simon Peter) but amazingly God had prompted me to read verses that were talking to me – Simon.

I have since learned that the Holy Spirit makes the Bible come alive, and God really does speak to us personally when we read its powerful words (See chapter five, "God Speaks".).

Over the coming weeks, my questions became ones marked more by seeking than by objections.

In June 1991, I went to a Cambridge University ball with a girlfriend at the time, and on a Sunday morning, I decided to ask Jesus to be my Lord and Saviour. I was unchurched and didn't know how to pray. I did know that I had to repent of rejecting God all my life. I said to Him that I still didn't understand where dinosaurs fitted in and why there was poverty in the world, but I did want Jesus in my life. And when I said those simple words, "Lord, I want You in my life", I was filled with that emotional, spiritual and physical feeling that I had when the wise man prayed for me in Bicester. It was such an incredible sense of being filled with love, peace and overwhelming joy that I fell to my knees and wept happy tears.

I have been a Christian ever since and my understanding of God, myself and the world has been transformed. The Holy Spirit really does open your eyes so you can see things differently.

A few weeks after asking Jesus into my life, I was mowing the lawn at my new house in Aylesbury and as I mowed, I prayed. In particular, I realised it was time to find a church, but I didn't know anything about the different types of churches and how to choose one. So I asked God to show me the church He wanted me to attend. A few minutes later, my new neighbour George popped his head over the garden fence, and we got chatting.

Suddenly he looked at his watch and apologised. "Sorry, I've got to rush," he said. "It's time to get to church."

"Can I come?" I responded. I knew that God had immediately answered my prayer for guidance for a church and Holy Trinity, Aylesbury became my first church and was where Clare and I eventually got married. I soon discovered that one of the vicars from the church also lived at the end of my road.

I can see now that God worked His plan out for me at the perfect time. He knew when my heart would become responsive to Him, and He placed people around me to start my Christian faith journey. He planted the thought about Easter and prompted me to read the Bible. He placed Andy in my life at work and He surrounded me with Christian neighbours who helped me start my church life.

God is a good God who has a plan for each one of us, and I am so thankful that He reached out to me and opened my eyes to who He is. My life has been enriched ever since, and I couldn't imagine surviving the ups and downs of life without His guidance and blessing.

Chapter 2
Jesus: Fact or Fiction?

"I have seen and I testify that this is God's Chosen One."
– John 1:34

I have always loved reading, particularly historical fiction and adventure stories by authors like Wilbur Smith and Conn Iggulden. When I was young, I read about King Arthur and his knights of the Round Table and enjoyed the mythical tales of the Greek gods.

As an atheist, I assumed that the stories in the Bible and, in particular, those about Jesus were the same genre. Fantasy! Interestingly, I had this belief, having never read a Bible or investigated whether what it said was true. I just dismissed it as myth without thought. According to the American Bible Society, over five hundred million Bibles are sold globally annually.[1] If it were included in the calculations, the Bible would top the best seller lists every year, and the trend is increasing. The Bible deserves investigation, and certainly, if you are going to suggest that it is full of fantasy, you should at least consider the evidence.

Over the last thirty years of reading the Bible and listening to sermons based on what it says, I have come to see it as "the" source of wisdom and guidance for life. My views and opinions were formerly shaped by the world I grew up in. Now, they are shaped by the Bible. If society says something today and it does not hold true with what I read in the Bible, then I will believe what the Bible says. A big example of this, which I will cover in the next chapter, is that I believe in a Creator. I no longer believe in evolution.

My consultancy business, Abacus International, assessed the evidence behind new drugs and medical devices. We mathematically modelled the economic impact of those healthcare products on national healthcare systems like the NHS. Our work influenced whether new drugs would get funded, and I firmly believe in making evidence-based decisions.

So, is my faith blind, or is it evidence-based?

I would say that my belief in God is absolutely evidence-based. I no longer think that you have to throw away reason and logic to believe in God. In fact, many of the greatest scientists in history were Christians[2]:

Michael Faraday, who discovered electromagnetic induction; Gregor Mendel, who founded the science of genetics; Blaise Pascal (probability theory); Allesandro Volta (the battery); Lord Kelvin (thermodynamics); Charles Babbage (father of the computer); Albrecht von Haller (father of modern physiology) and Samuel Morse (the telegraph) all believed in God. Isaac Newton, the father of calculus who discovered gravity and invented the telescope, was a passionate dissenting protestant who spent more time on Bible study than maths and physics.[3] There are many more, including modern-day scientists like Francis Collins, a geneticist who oversaw the Human Genome Project, one of the biggest research projects in history.

Incredibly clever scientists believe in God and the Jesus of the Bible. Faith and scientific thinking do not have to be mutually exclusive. You can have both, and my former views as an atheist were wrong.

There are different types of evidence, and science is just one discipline. Science tries to explain the "how." It does not explain the "why." Science is based on assumptions and projections that change over time as more "knowledge" is gained. In fact, science constantly creates more questions. We discover something, and that leads to another research question. Scientific belief can hold for centuries until it is disproved and replaced by another hypothesis. For example, it was believed that the Earth was the centre of the universe until Nicholas Copernicus, a catholic canon, mathematician and astronomer, discovered that it orbits around the sun, along with all the other planets in our solar system.

We have to accept that science cannot answer all questions, and that is particularly relevant when you consider the supernatural and the spiritual. I have no problem accepting that God is above the laws of science. He is outside time. He can change the laws of physics if He chooses. He can do things miraculously that cannot be explained scientifically. In the Bible, the people in the stories before the great flood of Noah's time seemed to live for hundreds of years. Today, the oldest person might live to one hundred and twenty years. I have no issue accepting that in the course of human history, God could choose to redefine human lifespans.

Consider this scientific definition:

"The anatomical juxtaposition of two orbicularis oris muscles in a state of contraction." What does it mean?

It describes a kiss, but can you see that there is so much missing from that scientific explanation? It doesn't capture the idea of love, which is an emotional and spiritual experience.

Experiential Evidence

Experiential evidence is hugely powerful. I am hoping to describe my personal experiences of God as a form of proof. My faith has grown enormously over thirty years because of a series of experiences. Answers to prayer, miracles, a sense of peace and sometimes a tingling feeling in my fingers when I feel the power of God's Spirit engulf me. I have had so many life "coincidences", or should I say God-incidences, that He has become real to me. One hundred percent real. I have no doubts left, and I know what will happen to me when I die. That is hugely comforting. I don't always understand what God is doing, and I am happy not to understand because I trust that He knows what He is doing.

I could describe the properties of water to you from a physical perspective. I could scientifically or mathematically prove that you will float if you get into our pool. However, you won't fully believe or trust me until you get in and find out that it is true. That is how it is with God. You have to repent and turn to Him, and then you find your experience of Him grows daily until you find yourself knowing that He is there, not as an intellectual idea, but specifically present, interacting in your life.

There is nothing more powerful than a personal experience of God to prove to you that He exists. I pray that you meet Him in whatever way is right for you.

Historical Evidence

Another hugely important type of evidence is historical. Do you believe in Julius Caesar, Alexander the Great, or a myriad of other historical characters? Do you believe the stories that are told about them? If so, why?

Historians will rate the quality of historical evidence through something called textual criticism. The closer to the date of the event and the more copies of the documented evidence, the better. A first-hand account is better than a second-hand one.

Even better if many written accounts describe the same event but with differences shaped by different perspectives and viewpoints. A single description of an event could be unreliable or biased.

I have recently read a fantastic book called, "Is Jesus History?" by John Dickson[4] and he uses the example of Alexander the Great to explain these principles. We know that Alexander the Great (356–323 BC) was the son of Philip the First and Olympias, King and Queen of Macedonia. In 334 BC, he set off to conquer the world and campaigned for around ten years. He had forty-three thousand soldiers and five thousand cavalry. We know which countries he conquered, which battles he fought, who his generals were and how he died. But how do we know this?

John Dickson points out that the bulk of our information comes from written sources composed after Alexander's death and copied over centuries in manuscripts stored in museums and libraries ever since. Numerous officials recorded accounts of Alexanders' exploits, but none of the early manuscripts exist today. Later writers referred to these early accounts, so we only have third-party references. The best of these was written by a philosopher called Arrian in the second century AD; there are thirty-six copies of that manuscript today. They were copied from a source manuscript written in twelve hundred AD. So, our earliest historical document describing Alexander the Great was written four hundred years after the events described, and it references the remarks of Polybius, who wrote one hundred and twenty years after Alexander's death.

Compare that to the Gospels in the Bible, which give a biographical account of Jesus. Mark was written within forty years of Jesus' crucifixion, Luke and Matthew within fifty years, and John within seventy years. All were written far closer to the events described than those of Alexander the Great.

John Dickson quotes Stanley Porter, who is a leader in the field of ancient manuscripts, and he states that "there are approximately five thousand five hundred manuscripts of the New Testament, a number larger than any other ancient Greek or Latin author or book."

He concludes, "The writings about Jesus are the best-attested records from all classical history."

No sane historian could argue that Jesus of Nazareth did not exist, and I am embarrassed by my early opinion about Jesus and the Bible that was based on ignorance rather than considered evidence.

Testimonial Evidence

In a court of law, the primary evidence used to decide whether someone is guilty or not is the testimony of witnesses and character references. Science (DNA testing) might aid the process but the primary evidence is personal testimony. That is what the Bible is full of, the testimony about Jesus the Messiah from various individuals who either met Jesus directly or spoke with people who had. Each of these different characters writes their version of events.

Simon Peter was a fisherman who observed all that Jesus did first-hand. So was John, who was Jesus' best friend. His Gospel focuses very much on the spiritual. Matthew, another Apostle, was a tax collector who gave more of a biographical account to prove to Jewish readers that Jesus was the promised Messiah who fulfilled the Old Testament prophecies. Mark was an assistant to the apostle Paul, accompanying him on his first missionary journey. He writes for unbelievers in a dramatic and emotional style. Luke was a doctor by profession and a gentile (non-Jewish). Again, he travelled around with Paul and wrote with the eye of a historian, documenting the facts. Paul was an academic theologian and would have made a good lawyer. He started off persecuting Christians until an encounter with Jesus changed his life. James was Jesus' half-brother.

I love that the Bible is a set of books written by over forty authors, all with a slightly different perspective, but together giving a comprehensive account of Jesus' life and teaching. Sometimes there are slight discrepancies but that adds to the authenticity of the texts. It would be suspicious if every eyewitness gave precisely the same account. Even the Old Testament (written before Jesus was born) points to Him.

The Evidence of Prophetic Fulfilment

My confidence in the Bible as a whole has grown when I compare its prophetic writings with real historical events. About eighty per cent of Biblical prophecy has already happened, and the rest is about the end of the world and Jesus' second coming, an unknown time in the future that is still to come. If someone made lots of claims about the future and they kept coming true, eventually you would believe them when they talk about something yet to occur. That is how I am with the Bible.

There are some amazingly specific examples of fulfilled biblical prophecy.

For example, Jeremiah warned the Israelites that they were going to be taken into captivity by the Babylonians (Jeremiah 25). He said that, after seventy years, Babylon itself would be conquered, and the Jews would be returned to Israel. One hundred and fifty years earlier, Isaiah also prophesied about this same event (Isaiah 45) and claimed that a king called Cyrus would conquer Babylon and return the Jews home. History tells us that it was King Cyrus of Persia who fulfilled this very specific prophecy in 538 BC.

In 614 BC, the prophet Nahum said that Nineveh would be damaged by fire (Nahum 3:15). Archaeologists unearthed the site during the eighteen hundreds and found a layer of ash covering the ruins. The city was sacked by the Babylonians, Scythians and Medes in 612 BC, just two years after the prophecy was made.

In 538 BC, the prophet Daniel wrote, "So you are to know and discern that from the issuing of a decree to restore and rebuild Jerusalem until Messiah the Prince there will be seven weeks of years and sixty-two weeks of years" (Daniel 9:25).

On 5 March 444 BC, Artaxerxes, a Persian King, published a decree to restore Jerusalem (Nehemiah 2:1).

On 30 March 33 AD, Jesus rode into Jerusalem on a donkey and was declared Messiah (Luke 19:38–40).

Amazingly, that is precisely the amount of time that Daniel prophesied (sixty-nine weeks of years).[5]

So many of the Old Testament prophecies about the Messiah were fulfilled by Jesus. He was born to a virgin and from a specific genealogical lineage (Abraham, Jesse, Jacob, David and Judah). He was born in Bethlehem but raised in Egypt. His coming was foretold by a messenger (John the Baptist). He was betrayed by a friend (Judas) for thirty pieces of silver. His hands and feet were pierced during crucifixion and yet the normal process of breaking His bones did not happen. He was crucified alongside two criminals and yet assigned the grave of a rich man. He was resurrected after three days. These very specific fulfilled prophecies give me confidence that Jesus was the foretold Messiah.

There are hundreds of Biblical prophecies that we can demonstrate have come true, and the only ones left are the ones about the end of the world. We will look at those later.

If you are interested in the details of the prophecies about the Messiah that Jesus fulfilled, then study the Appendix at the end of this book.

So to conclude this chapter: Can a rational person believe in God? The answer is "yes"! Is believing in Jesus evidence-based? Absolutely! The historical evidence in the Gospels is the best of all available ancient manuscripts. In determining spiritual truth, science and maths are the wrong disciplines to use. We have lots of written testimonies recording what people saw and experienced. Just like in a court of law, you have to consider those accounts before deciding whether they speak the truth.

Reading the biblical evidence and hearing Andy's personal testimony was enough for me to take a step of faith and ask Jesus into my life. Since then, my personal experiences have left me with a deep certainty that God is real, and I pray that you will reach the same conclusion.

Chapter 3
Accident or Design?

"The wrath of God is being revealed from Heaven against all the godlessness and wickedness of people, who suppress the truth by their wickedness since what may be known about God is plain to them, because God has made it plain to them. For since the creation of the world God's invisible qualities – His eternal power and divine nature – have been clearly seen, being understood from what has been made, so that people are without excuse."

– Romans 1:18–20

As I said in the introduction, for many years I was a card-carrying evolutionist who had written a thesis studying the concepts of adaptation and survival of the fittest. I believed that life emerged from single cells and that man and apes evolved from a common ancestor over billions of years. I also thought that the concept of a Creator was foolish and only for the feeble-minded. I would have been at home in the Richard Dawkins camp.

How my mindset has changed since asking Jesus into my life! The Holy Spirit fills us and changes how we think and see things, and I now fully believe in a God who created everything. I know Christians who somehow try to compromise and accept both God and the theory of evolution. I don't think you can. Either a Creator created all things, or it all occurred by chance through evolution.

Most people accept the Big Bang at the start of time. I can quite imagine a huge explosion that flung the stars into space, and it makes me marvel at God's power and glory. The Big Bang was God's doing, not just a random evolutionary moment.

But I also believe in a God who created everything in six days and rested on the seventh. To reject that idea in favour of a gradual evolution over billions of years is to not fully grasp our Creator God's unbelievable majesty and power.

I'd also like to say at this stage that for those who accept the theory of evolution and the estimations of the age of the Earth, it is also an act of faith. You are putting your trust in the calculations and theories of various scientists.

Let me claim as a logical and scientific person that believing in a Creator makes so much more sense than accepting that life occurred through random chance over billions of years.

Imagine a painting like the Mona Lisa. Here are two different arguments as to how that painting came to be. Argument one is that paint was thrown billions of times at a canvas until, eventually, it randomly fell in the correct pattern to form Mona Lisa's face.

Argument two is that an artist called Leonardo De Vinci painted that face through the careful application of different coloured paints and with exceptional skill and creativity.

It would be bonkers to believe theory one, wouldn't it? When you look at a painting, you also see something about the artist behind it. I visited a Van Gogh exhibition in London a couple of years ago, and it presented the different paintings he had made during various stages of his life. You could definitely learn something about the artist and what he was going through in life through the paintings. His later works when he was in an asylum for mental health problems were completely different from his earlier works when in Holland.

Imagine a watch consisting of thirty to fifty cogs, coils and bits of glass. Which theory is more believable? We put the parts in a bag and shake them up randomly billions of times, and eventually, they fall together perfectly to make a working watch. Or there was a Master watchmaker in Switzerland who painstakingly crafted that watch into a working timepiece.

The random chance theory is illogical in comparison to the crafted and designed theory, isn't it? So why then, when we look at the universe, vastly more complicated than a watch or a painting, do we throw out logic and choose the random chance rather than Creator theory?

The Scripture I used to head this Chapter tells us that we are meant to see the Creator when we look at creation. God says that He has made it plain to all people through His creation that He, the Creator, exists. We can see His eternal power and divine nature when we look at the world and the universe we live in. No person has an excuse to reject God when they see the stunning masterpiece of His creation.

Have you ever sat on your own quietly in nature? I find that I am filled with a great sense of peace when I am in the great outdoors. My daily troubles seem to become smaller as I ponder the beauty of creation and my insignificance in the grand scheme of things. That sense of peace in nature is because we are in some way communing with God, the Creator. It was what mankind was designed to do: to walk with God in the beautiful garden of Eden. He made this Earth and our universe for you and me to enjoy. That boggles my mind. An all-powerful Creator God who made all things, including the animals and plants, for our pleasure. He wants you and I to enjoy being with Him in the beauty of His creation, and we taste a little of that when we go for a walk in nature.

When I see the complexity of creation, I now marvel at the power of my Creator God.

I bought a telescope a few years ago, and what surprised me was instead of just making the moon look bigger, it turned the night sky from a few visible stars to a glittering mass of them.

There are many different estimates of how big space is, and these change over time, but a recent one I found online suggested that the Milky Way galaxy, of which our solar system is just a part, contains between one hundred and four hundred billion stars.[6] Researchers say that the Milky Way is just one of between one hundred and five hundred billion galaxies. The absolute number of stars is too great for our minds to comprehend, greater than the number of grains of sand on Earth.[7] When I think upon such things, I marvel at the power of our Almighty God, who spoke all of this into being.

With all those stars and planets, some ponder whether there are life forces elsewhere. Aliens.

I don't believe in aliens because I think that God has created mankind as His special possession. He created

Earth perfectly for us – the right atmosphere and a tilted axis of twenty three point four degrees that creates the seasons. Any closer to the sun, the Earth would be too hot to sustain life; any further away, we would be too cold.

I find it amazing that every leaf on every tree is different. God could have created an oak tree with a specific template leaf type that was all the same. Instead, he chooses each tree to have a unique mix of leaves. There are nearly eight billion people on Earth, and we all have unique fingerprints, faces and DNA. We all have unique personalities, shapes, sizes and colours. All made in the image of God, similar but unique.

Let me say it again: we are meant to see God when we are in His Creation.

Whenever I am at an ocean looking at amazing blue seas and the never-ending action of the waves, I see my eternal Creator God.

I have stood at Niagara and Victoria Falls and seen the immense surge of water pouring over the precipice, and I think about my all-powerful Creator.

When I see a beautiful sunset or sunrise, I praise God.

I have stood in the freezing cold on a glacier in Iceland. It glows a deep blue, and of course, the Northern Lights are a spectacular cosmic experience. God is everywhere when you choose to look.

My closest encounters with God have been sitting on top of mountains, looking at the fantastic views (more of that in a later chapter).

I love safaris and have had some amazing encounters with wild animals. The huge elephants seem so otherworldly; the beautiful Kingfishers and the bright yellow weaverbirds building their upside-down nests. I have sat within five feet of a lion roaring to its brothers at night – an absolutely terrifying sound! The ugly scavengers like the vultures and hyenas and, of course, the monkeys in their various forms, from the tiny vervets with their cute little faces to the baboons with their big pink bottoms!

The vast variety of animal and plant life all points to a highly imaginative Creator, and the complexity of ecosystems and how they all fit together is marvellous. Mankind is sustained by the vast range of animals and plants. We need the insects for pollination. We need some of the animals and plants to eat. We need photosynthesis to create the right atmosphere for us to survive in. We need trees for shade and to recycle carbon dioxide. We need the fish in the seas and the birds in the sky. Our God is good, and He has created everything to meet our needs and many things to give us pleasure.

So, let's talk about the theory of Evolution. It is what it says: a theory created by Charles Darwin in 1859 after travelling the world on his boat, the Beagle. I think that this theory has caused more damage to mankind's relationship with and understanding of God than anything else in modern-day culture. It forms a stumbling block for so many (me included in my first twenty-six years), and it is so often presented wrongly on TV and in schools as fact.

The Bible tells us that God created all kinds of creatures. I can understand that Darwin was amazed when he saw the variety of life, and when he saw monkeys with faces a bit like the man, he invented this eloquent, but what I believe is a wrong theory. Apparently, mankind shares ninety-eight percent of its genes with chimpanzees. That does not prove that they evolved from a common ancestor. It simply says that God chose for man and apes to have a similar genome. We share fifty percent of our genes with a banana. That does not mean that you and I are half bananas! It just means that God chose for us to share fifty percent of our genes.

When I did my biology studies, we were taught about adaptation and survival of the fittest as driving forces for evolution. A typical example used is one of black and white moths. Initially, the white moth predominates. When industrialisation happened, trees and landscapes became polluted with soot, and the background environment got darker. A genetic accident occurred, and black moths "evolved" from white ones. Because the white moth is more easily spotted against a dark backdrop, they begin to die out, and now the black moth predominates. Adaptation, followed by survival of the fittest, drives the development of new species.

I have no problem saying that God created many different creatures and when the environment changes, some of the species He created die out whilst others thrive. We are polluting the Earth at a great rate right now, and many species are dying out.

Most dog breeds we know today have been bred for particular characteristics. That kind of genetic evolution is not a problem. God created wolves and dogs, and they have changed their characteristics through breeding. That's fine. The problem comes when you use this method to drive the concept of speciation. The idea is that everything that exists on earth, including all the different kinds of species, initially started from a single cell. Eventually, over billions of years, one cell became multicellular organisms, which in turn became sea creatures who, when they adapted for land, became animals and eventually birds and, of course, at the end of the process, mankind.

Question: What was there in the beginning, and how do you go from nothing to something? Our minds are not big enough to answer this. I find it easy to accept that God was there always. I don't need to understand eternity; I accept the following scripture: "In the beginning was the Word, and the Word was with God, and the Word was God. He was with God in the beginning. Through Him all things were made; without Him nothing was made that has been made. In Him was life, and that life was the light of all mankind" (John 1:1–4).

Question: Where did the first living cell come from? No one has been able to replicate an experiment where a living cell was created from organic inert chemicals. Scientists accept now that even a single cell is unbelievably complicated. It could not have just appeared by accident. God is the Author of life.

Question: Why are crossbreeds generally infertile? You can breed successfully within a species, like a dog with a dog, but when you try to go too far, the resulting creature is infertile. So, for example, if you breed a horse with a donkey, you get an ass or a mule. These are infertile, so the process of speciation breaks down. God has set limits on what can breed with what.

Question: Where is the missing link in the supposed evolution of man? The idea in the survival of the fittest is that animal version B is more suited to the environment than version A, so A dies out and B survives. Then C evolves, and so B dies out, and then version D evolves, and C dies out, and so on. Eventually, you claim that man (version G, for example) evolved from ape (version A). If this is the case, why are ape and man still present but none of the intermediate steps? God chose to create man and apes. I now believe that evolution is wrong.

I sometimes get irritated by what I hear claimed on nature and human biology programmes because foolish things are said in the name of evolution. There was a slightly controversial TV programme a few years ago that covered human life from conception to death. It was controversial because it filmed the process of the death of a sick man. The first programme, talking about the birth process, claimed that if the human baby had not evolved a soft fontanelle, then birth could not have happened.

Basically, it was saying that babies have a soft front and back part of the head, enabling them to pass through the mother's birth canal. These soft parts of the head harden up over time, the back fontanelle after two months and the front one after seven to eighteen months. Think about it. Evolution requires live birth in order to work. You can't get a genetic improvement that makes an advantageous adaptation that drives survival of the fittest without a live birth. The soft fontanelle cannot have evolved. It was designed by God, our cosmic Physician and Physiologist.

I once watched a programme about dinosaurs. The amount of assumptive language was unbelievable: words like "could have", "possibly", "might have". The programme was littered with the scientists making up all sorts of theories. Yes, dinosaurs existed and yes, we can piece together ideas of how they lived, what they ate and where they lived. But let's not forget that much of what scientists say is assumptive.

Even the calculations of the age of the universe are highly assumptive and do not take into account the idea of a supernatural God who can do things outside the laws of physics.

Take radioactive carbon dating, for example. If we know that a radioactive substance decays at a particular rate and measure the amount of that substance in a rock today, we can back-calculate the age of the rock. This method contains some basic assumptions that the decay rate has always been the same. It also assumes that the substance started at a place of zero decay. Having had a career in mathematical modelling, I know that if you change a few critical assumptions in a mathematical model by just a tiny amount, you get a completely different answer. That's why scientists have changed the estimates of the age of the universe by billions of years in modern scientific history.

The idea of God creating everything in six days is no more fanciful than the theory that everything was made from nothing via a process of evolution over billions of years. In fact, I find the idea of a Creator behind everything that is created so much more logical than a theory of design by accident.

I believe the account of the Garden of Eden. I believe that God literally created Adam, the first man. Genesis describes that the garden had four rivers flowing through it. Two of them, the Tigris and the Euphrates, still exist today. They wind through modern-day Turkey, Iraq and Syria before emptying into the Persian Gulf. In ancient geography, these rivers created what we think of as the fertile crescent in ancient Mesopotamia. The Bible says that Adam and Eve were evicted from the Garden of Eden, so they and their family would have settled along the fertile crescent created by these great rivers. Ancient geography tells us that the world's first urban civilisations began to develop in southern Mesopotamia (now Iraq).[8] The lower Euphrates river plains have been farmed since 6200 BC and by 3500 BC farming communities were growing into the world's first towns and cities such as Ur where Abraham came from.

I no longer believe that ape-like creatures evolved into man in Africa and then populated the Earth. I now believe that God created Adam, and he and his descendants spread out to populate the Earth, starting from the fertile crescent. Go South, and man would be in Africa. Go North-East and he would populate Asia and beyond. Go North-West and he would populate Europe.

Mitochondrial DNA (MtDNA) testing traces people's ancient maternal ancestry from one to two hundred thousand years ago. It goes back to a single woman from whom all humans are believed to have inherited their mitochondrial DNA, known as Mitochondrial Eve.

Scientific disciplines support the biblical account rather than disproving it.

I believe that the biblical account of the flood is a totally plausible explanation of the fossil record and could account for the extinction of species like the dinosaurs.

For me, the saddest aspect of the evolution story is that its central message is the opposite of what God wants you to know. Evolution says that you are an accident of nature and are descended from an ape. You are a product of chance and just another animal. It tells you that there is no purpose to life other than to survive and be in competition with others for resources. When you die, your chemical components will simply be recycled. This is so far from the biblical message. You are a son or daughter of the King of Kings and He loves you with an eternal passion. God has created you for a purpose and He designed a beautiful world for you to enjoy and look after. When your body dies, your spirit will live on into eternity. He wants to spend that eternity with you.

Let me conclude this chapter. We are meant to see the nature of the Creator when we look at His creation. I don't think that science and faith are incompatible. Science as a discipline tries to interpret the evidence before us, but it has limits to what it can explain and sometimes science is wrong in its assumptions. Now, when I look at the magnificence of the universe and the complexity of life, instead of putting it all down to a scientific accident, I marvel at the power and majesty of my Lord God.

Chapter 4
Who is God?

"In the beginning was the Word, and the Word was with God, and the Word was God. He was with God in the beginning. Through Him all things were made; without Him nothing was made that has been made. In Him was life, and that life was the light of all mankind. The light shines in the darkness, and the darkness has not overcome it."
– John 1:1–5

As an atheist, I had never really thought beyond a vague intellectual concept that God was some kind of Higher Power that some people believed in.

Now, I understand that He is a real person, someone I have a personal relationship with, someone I talk to every day and someone I cannot imagine living without. He is as real and important to me as my wife Clare or my three daughters. I depend on Him for everything and trust Him with my future. He is the first person I turn to when life is tough or when I am feeling anxious about something, and He fills me with His peace just when I need it.

Sadly, too many people see God, if they believe in Him at all, as a faraway, unapproachable Being who is uninterested in their lives. According to them, He is a Deity to be obeyed and to be scared of and someone who will punish you if you do something wrong.

That is so far from the truth, and it is the reason for Jesus – who is God made known. God made humanity so we can grasp who He is and hear that He loves us and wants to be in our lives.

Let me try to explain a difficult concept – the Trinity (a term that is not found specifically anywhere in the Bible but has been used by Christians down the centuries to describe God's nature). Christians believe in one God in the form of three persons: Father, Son and Holy Spirit. Our minds are too small to fully grasp how one being can also be three, and that's OK. The closest I can get is that a chemical element can be in the form of a solid, liquid or gas. It's the same element, just in a different state. That is too simplistic because the three people of the Trinity speak to each other as if they are separate individuals.

Let's take them one at a time.

God the Father

God has various names that give us a richer understanding of who He is.

Yahweh, or Jehovah, is the name for the God of the Israelites, and it represents the biblical pronunciation of "YHWH," the Hebrew name revealed to Moses in the book of Exodus. It means "I am who I am" and indicates that God is the source of everything. We have considered God as Creator in chapter three.

We also call Him "The Almighty". This name refers to His unimaginable power and might and can inspire fear. To some extent, we should fear Him. The Bible says that "the fear of God is the beginning of wisdom" (Proverbs 9:10). The Jews could not look at God without falling to the floor and covering their eyes for fear of dying. Even their High Priest was not allowed into the Holy of Holies, the inner sanctuary of the Tabernacle where God would appear, other than once a year on a special feast day.

God is Holy. That means "set apart". There is no one else in the universe like the living-God. He is pure and perfect and calls us to be pure and perfect. As One who is holy, God hates sin and any kind of wickedness. In the Old Testament, we see a God of wrath who destroyed cities like Sodom and Gomorrah because of their wickedness (Genesis 19). We are told that in the future, He will punish sinners and confine them to an eternity in Hell (more of that in a later chapter). Too many people see Him as "God All Matey" rather than God Almighty and, therefore, do not live lives in reverent fear of Him.

The Hebrews called Him El Elyon, "God Most High," and El Roi, "The God who Sees". It reminds us that God is above everything and is all-seeing. There is nothing that goes on in our lives, good or bad, that God does not see. He is all-knowing and all-wise. There is nothing that has ever happened in history or nothing that will happen in the future that He does not know about.

There are also lovely Hebrew terms like Jehovah Jireh, "God My Provider," and Jehovah Nissi, "The Lord is My Banner," that describe other aspects of God's character and how He relates to us.

My favourite term, though, is "Abba Father". It is an Aramaic term for an intimate relationship with your dad. My heart melts when my daughters call me, "Daddy". I feel overwhelmed by the intimacy of that term. I am "Daddy" to three beautiful girls whom I adore. That is one of the aspects of God that I particularly relate to. He is all loving and cares so deeply about each one of us. When we pray the Lord's prayer, it is "Abba Father", "Daddy", to whom we pray.

So how can an all-loving Abba Father also be a God of wrath who judges and punishes and hates sin of any kind? How can He be perfectly just and perfectly loving at the same time?

The reason He hates sin is that it is so damaging. It prevents us from coming into His Holy presence and ultimately keeps us from entering heaven. The consequences of sin hurt us, His precious children. God hates seeing our greed that is polluting the planet He created perfectly. He hates seeing the unequal distribution of wealth that creates poverty in some parts of the world. He hates seeing people ruining their lives through addiction or others who have lost all sense of identity. He hates hearing the cruel things we say about each other. When you discipline your child, you are actually showing love as a parent. You are helping them learn a lesson that will avoid damaging behaviour in the future. You are shaping them into a better human being for their own good. That is what God longs to do as He calls us away from sin (a life turned in on ourselves), and calls us towards knowing and loving Him (a life turned outward and upward).

Imagine a judge seeing his brother come before him because he has committed a crime. The perfectly just judge has to condemn the brother he loves and punish him accordingly. But as a loving brother, the judge then removes his robes and pays the penalty that his brother should have shouldered. Crime has to be punished. Love pays the price.

That is where Jesus, the Son of God, comes in.

God the Son

Jesus, too, has several names. The one we think of at Christmas is Immanuel, which means "God with us". The concept is that God sees the mess the world is getting into and intervenes by sending His Son to be born as fully human and fully God at the same time. God himself comes to Earth, and we read Jesus' mission statement in John 3:16–18,

"For God so loved the world that He gave His one and only Son, that whoever believes in Him shall not perish but have eternal life. For God did not send His Son into the world to condemn the world, but to save the world through Him. Whoever believes in Him is not condemned, but whoever does not believe stands condemned already because they have not believed in the name of God's one and only Son" (John 3:16–18).

Another name is "Messiah", which means Saviour. Christians often talk about being saved by Jesus, but that doesn't explain what we are being saved from. I will say more on this later, but in simplest terms, we need to be saved from ourselves, because our sins lead to death and ultimately to life without God: Hell. The things we are being saved from have to be enormous because the solution (Jesus' death on a cross) is drastic.

We often think that the term Christ is Jesus' surname. It actually means the Anointed One. So His full name means the "Anointed One Who Saves". Jesus Christ was chosen by God the Father to save people from their sins and therefore from death.

Two of my favourite worship songs are "King of Kings" and "Above all Powers", which remind us that there is no authority in Heaven and on Earth greater than Jesus. Everyone has to come under His control, even Satan. The Bible tells us that at the name of Jesus, every knee will bow, and every tongue will confess Him as Lord (Philippians 2:10–11). This bowing will either be in adoration, or in fear and trembling, because we are also told that God has appointed Jesus as judge at the end of time.

I remember, as a student, the numerous times I had to queue up at a notice board to see my exam results. Each time was a nerve-wracking experience, as you felt like your future depended on the results. Can you imagine what it would feel like if the adjudication was whether you lived or died? You would spend a lot of time revising and trying to understand what the judge was going to base His judgment upon (more of that in chapter seven).

Jesus is also called the Lamb of God and this term is slightly more difficult to explain unless you understand some Old Testament basics. Sin has consequences and requires a penalty to be paid. In order to "atone" for their sin, (i.e. make themselves right with God), the Israelites had to pay the price with blood. Every morning and evening a lamb would be sacrificed ceremonially for the sins of the people.

Another important Jewish ceremony is Passover, which celebrates the time when the Israelites escaped slavery in Egypt. God told Moses to instruct the Israelites to paint their doors with the blood of a pure, unblemished lamb, so that the angel of death that was sent to kill all firstborn children in Egypt would pass over that house. This was the final "plague" sent to Pharoah to persuade him to let the Jews go (Exodus 12).

It is no accident that Jesus was crucified during the week of Passover. He replaced the Jewish Passover meal with the Last Supper and what we now think of as Communion. He also replaced the need for daily sacrifice for the atonement of sin by becoming the once for all sacrificial lamb. His death on the cross paid for the sins of all mankind in one act. There is now no more need for daily animal sacrifices because the ultimate death penalty has been paid.

This all sounds quite complicated. All you need to understand is that when we reject God, we are sinning, and that leads to the death penalty, which has to be paid. A perfectly just God pronounces the sentence of death but then a perfectly loving Jesus steps in and takes on Himself the punishment we deserve. This way both justice and mercy are shown.

Jesus is described as the Alpha and the Omega, the beginning and the end (Revelation 1:8), reminding us that He was there at the beginning before Creation with God the Father and will be there at the end of time.

We are told that He is now at the right hand of the Father, interceding for each one of us. He is like our defence attorney, pleading our case before His Father.

Let's look at what Jesus said about Himself.

- I am the Bread of Life (John 6:35): Jesus alone can sustain us spiritually. He is food for the soul and without Him, we will remain spiritually hungry.

- I am the Light of the World (John 8:12): The world is a dark place full of unhappiness. Jesus brings light and hope into that darkness. We are told at the end of time that the sun and stars will stop shining and that Jesus will literally be our light source.

- I am the Gate (or Door) of the Sheepfold (John 10:7): Jesus is the exclusive entrance to abundant life. Through Him, we find safety, protection and access to God's grace.

- I am the Good Shepherd (John 10:11, 14): I particularly like this term as it sums up His role as a protector and provider. He is someone who feeds His sheep, who chases after them when they get lost and who fends off the wild animals who prey on them. I definitely see Jesus as my Shepherd who guides every step of my life.

- I am the Resurrection and the Life (John 11:25): Jesus declares His power over death. He is the source of eternal life and promises resurrection to all who believe in Him. We need to investigate the truth of the resurrection, as everything else in Christianity hinges on it.

- I am the Way, the Truth and the Life (John 14:6): This is a key scripture that we will examine in the chapter on different religions. It's a big claim, isn't it? Jesus says He is the only way to God the Father, the only way to eternal salvation, the only way to Heaven.

- I am the True Vine (John 15:1): Jesus compares Himself to a vine, and believers are the branches. Our life and fruitfulness depend on remaining connected to Him. We are told that we need to abide in Him. When we are not connected to Jesus spiritually, our lives are empty and barren.

The reason He was tried by the Jewish religious leaders and ultimately crucified was because of blasphemy. He claimed to be able to forgive sins. Only God can do that.

So, was Jesus God? Some people claim that He was just a wise teacher and a good man. Based on what Jesus claimed about Himself, I don't think that option exists.

There are only three options[9]:

1. He was mad... He truly believed what He claimed but it was false.

2. He was bad... He knew that He was telling lies and deceiving people.

3. He was God... He was who He claimed to be.

We all need to decide what we believe.

I don't think any of the evidence suggests that He was mad. When Jesus was a little boy, He was found teaching the religious leaders in the temple. They were amazed at

His wisdom and knowledge. Throughout His three years of public ministry, crowds flocked to hear Him speak, and many just called Him "teacher".

It would also be mad to claim superpowers. Imagine if I told you that I could fly. I would be a laughing stock unless I demonstrated my superpower. Jesus warned His disciples that He would die but, after three days, would rise from the dead. He demonstrated that superpower. He prophesied that Judas would betray Him and he did. He prophesied that Jerusalem would be destroyed and that the Jews would be scattered around the earth. Rome destroyed Jerusalem forty years later, around 70 AD, and we know that the Jews remained scattered until after World War Two, when the nation of Israel was re-created.

Nothing about Jesus suggests "madman".

When you read about the life of Jesus, does He come across as a bad man? He taught "love your neighbour". He taught about how to love and how to live in peace with one another. He healed people. He cried when His friend died and raised three people from the dead because He cared for the pain of their families. He stayed silent when He was unfairly tried and when He heard people bringing false testimony against Him. His teaching was full of wisdom and love; people would have recognised Him as a gentle and humble man. He challenged religious hypocrisy.

Is there anything recorded about His life that suggests that He was a bad man? The Bible answers this question with a definitive "no!".

That only leaves one option. He was who He claimed to be and who the prophets of old had said would come. He demonstrated that He was God through His miracles and through the wisdom of His teaching. He demonstrated His power over death. He fulfilled so many of the prophecies about the Messiah. He was born to a virgin. He was descended from King David of the line of Judah. He was born in Bethlehem but was rejected by His own people. He was betrayed for thirty pieces of silver. He died and was resurrected. His feet and hands were pierced but His bones were left intact. He was killed alongside wicked men but buried in the tomb of a rich man. All of these are prophecies that Jesus fulfilled.

I believe that Jesus is the Son of God, and my prayer is that you would come to accept this too.

God the Holy Spirit

As an atheist, I had heard about God and Jesus, but I had never given any thought to the third member of the Trinity, the Holy Spirit. I thought the story of Jesus finished at Easter when Jesus died and was raised to life, yet for us as Christians that is actually the beginning. Hundreds of people saw Jesus alive for forty days after the resurrection. He continued to eat with His disciples and continued to teach them.

In Acts 1, we read the following:

"On one occasion, while He was eating with them, He gave them this command: 'Do not leave Jerusalem but wait for the gift My Father promised, which you have heard Me speak about. For John baptized with water, but in a few days you will be baptised with the Holy Spirit'" (Acts 1:4–6).

Jesus promised them power when the Holy Spirit came upon them, and that happened just after the disciples watched Jesus ascend into the sky and through the clouds. The Holy Spirit gave them the ability to do the same things that Jesus had been doing. The disciples spread the Gospel in the power of the Holy Spirit. They healed and did other miracles just as Jesus had done. They were given the wisdom to teach even though several of them were simple fishermen.

At Pentecost, we are told that the Holy Spirit fell upon a crowd of three thousand people, and they were all filled with this power and supernaturally spoke in different tongues (languages).

The Holy Spirit has been at work in Christians ever since. He is our Counsellor. He gives us wisdom and helps us to make good decisions. When we turn to Jesus and repent, we are made clean, and the Holy Spirit comes to dwell in our hearts. He is the ultimate intimacy of God living in us. It was the Holy Spirit that put the thought in my mind during the Easter of 1991 to read the Bible to find the Easter story within it. It is the Holy Spirit who convicts us of sin. He makes us realise that we are in need of Jesus, the Saviour. He is our conscience, making us sensitive to our wrongdoings.

The Holy Spirit gently works on our characters to make us more like the person God designed us to be. He gives us the gift of discernment, knowing right from wrong. He is the manifestation of the love of God. When I asked Jesus to be my Saviour I was so filled with the Holy Spirit that I fell down on my knees in tears. He is the One who supernaturally fills us with peace and joy even when life is tough. The Holy Spirit washes away fear and anxiety.

He is the One who inspired the authors of the sixty-six books of the Bible to write what they wrote. He is the One who speaks personally to us when we read the Bible.

One day, a Jewish religious leader called Nicodemus asked Jesus what we have to do to get to Heaven, and this was his reply:

"Jesus answered, 'Very truly I tell you, no one can enter the kingdom of God unless they are born of water and the Spirit. Flesh gives birth to flesh, but the Spirit gives birth to spirit'" (John 3:5–6).

Jesus taught that in order to get to Heaven, we need to be born again. We are all born of water (in our mother's wombs), but we are spiritually dead. It is the Holy Spirit that makes us alive spiritually, and that process is called "being born again". Unfortunately this term has been taken by the modern media and turned into something that sounds like a cult. Lots of people who would call themselves Christians have not experienced the power that comes when you are born again and filled with the Holy Spirit. I think that it is vital when people are baptised in water ceremonies to also ask for the Holy Spirit to fill them. He makes such a massive difference in your life.

If you believe in Jesus but do not think that you are born again, you need to ask for the Holy Spirit to fill you. It is something I do regularly. The process is simple. Sin prevents us hearing from God and receiving the Holy

Spirit. We have to repent and then ask Jesus into our lives. Once He has forgiven us, He has washed us clean inside and out. Then, we are able to receive the Holy Spirit and be filled with this wonderful intimacy of God's power at work within us.

Let me share a powerful experience I had when I was a young Christian. I was playing piano in a church service where a visiting Pentecostal preacher was speaking about giving everything we are to God. At the end, I was playing the last worship song as people went forward for prayer. This visiting pastor pointed at me and said that I was to come forward. As he asked the Holy Spirit to fill me, I found myself saying to God, "Everything I have, Lord, all my money, my time, my skills, every cell in my body is Yours for the rest of my life."

At that point of total surrender to God, I was slain in the spirit. This is described in the Bible as falling over as you are overwhelmed by the Spirit of God. I felt like I was soaring and entirely at peace with the world and the next thing, I realised that I was lying on the carpet. It wasn't a faint as I was totally awake and aware. When Clare, my wife, first became a Christian, this happened to her regularly. It is an amazing experience to be utterly overcome by the Spirit of God.

In the next chapter, I will describe my experience of hearing from God. All these interactions with Him are through the Holy Spirit at work in my life.

Chapter 5
God Speaks

"For God does speak – now one way, now another – though no one perceives it."

– Job 33:14

I shared earlier that my first conversation with Andy at work was over him not drinking alcohol.

I was staggered when he answered, "God told me to stop." It seemed inconceivable as an atheist that God would speak to people. In fact, as atheists, we are choosing not to listen to Him, and our heart attitudes prevent us from hearing from Him.

My experiences over the last thirty years have inconclusively proven that God does indeed speak and that He is really there, intervening in every aspect of our lives.

God speaks in different ways, so let's start with the Bible, His handbook for living. It contains wisdom and instruction on every aspect of life, including how to develop your relationship with Him and how to get along with others. It helps us navigate right from wrong, and I use it to determine what God thinks versus what society thinks. Over the millennia, societies have changed, and what is deemed right or wrong has changed. Today, we sometimes feel that we are more enlightened than in the past, but the truth is that we have simply lowered the moral bar. What was not deemed acceptable fifty years ago is OK now. God is unchanging, and the Bible, for me, sets the moral standards by which I seek to live.

But the Bible is much more than just a set of moral codes. It is the living Word of God and it has been remarkable how the Holy Spirit has used specific words of Scripture to speak into my life over many years. Specific prayers get answered when reading the Bible, and I have made significant life decisions because of a word of Scripture that has been given to me.

Let me give you an example.

In 2011, I went on a mission trip to Eswatini in Southern Africa with some friends. I was running my healthcare consultancy company, Abacus International, and was really feeling the pressure of being a boss. I had over seventy staff members at the time and clients worldwide, and I felt the weight of responsibility of running what had become a multimillion-pound business.

On the trip, one of the leaders shared a scripture piece with us as part of a thought for the day, "Come to Me all you who are heavy burdened, and I will give you rest" (Matthew 11:28). It resonated with me. I was heavily burdened, and I did feel like I needed emotional rest from my responsibilities. Here was God saying, "I will give you rest." You know that He is speaking when what you are reading and hearing settles deeply in your heart. For the rest of that two-week trip, I met with HIV orphans; I saw people in utter poverty and I met teenage girls who had turned to prostitution as the only means to feed their younger siblings. My heart was broken by what I saw, but I also realised how blessed my life was. During that trip, I stopped thinking about my own pressures and problems as they paled into insignificance compared with those I met.

At the end of the mission trip, I found myself in the mountains in the north of Eswatini overlooking the border with Mozambique. I decided to get up at dawn to pray and to listen to God. This was to become a real mountaintop moment for me and changed the course of my life. I sat with my back to a wooden stake and watched the sun rise over the valley and lovely mountains. It is easier to hear from God when you are in His stunning creation and have left behind the clutter and noise of your life.

I felt like I was literally sitting at the foot of the cross and returned to the scripture about being heavily burdened. It went on to say, "Take My yoke upon you and learn from Me, for I am gentle and humble in heart, and you will find rest for your souls. For My yoke is easy and My burden is light" (Matthew 11:29–30). As I meditated on these words, I pictured a yoke. It is the device that goes around the neck of an ox to tether it to the cart or to another ox. As I prayed, I realised that I wanted to wear God's yoke with all of my heart. I wanted to serve Him with everything I had, and currently, I was wearing a different yoke – that of my business. An ox cannot wear two yokes as it would pull him in different directions. If I was going to wear God's yoke, I would have to take off the current one, that of Abacus.

An immense peace settled on me, so I knew that this was God's plan. I was going to go home and sell the company and see where God led me. He speaks powerfully through scripture.

But He also speaks into our thoughts. During that same mountaintop time in Eswatini, I had what can only be described as a video replay of my life. God showed me how much He had blessed me. He showed me my gentle and loving wife, my three beautiful daughters, my lovely home and my successful business. I felt humbled by the reminder of how much I was blessed compared to so many people, and then God showed me myself, how I turned His blessings into a curse by my wrong attitudes and words. I focused on the stress of running the company and feeling burdened rather than being joyful that I had such a successful business with loyal staff and clients.

He showed me the impact of me as a husband and father when I was at home and found the house a mess. I would get into a rage when trying to tidy up. I would quickly run out of patience when doing homework with the children or trying to teach them piano. My work stress was turning me into Mr Angry at home, and my cross words were harming my wife and daughters.

In this video replay, God showed me my real self, and I didn't like what I saw. I repented (asked God for forgiveness) in that moment on the mountain. The first thing I did when I arrived home a few days later was to put the bags down and apologise to Clare for my angry words and lack of patience. Something I didn't even realise was wrong in my marriage was healed in that moment. I also said sorry to my kids. When we listen to what God is saying, He can do mighty things in us.

About a year later, I had sold my business. I remember being at a school musical event when my phone pinged.

It was one of fourteen offers I received for Abacus and it was five times higher than anyone had expected because there was so much competitive interest in what we did. God had truly blessed the obedience of stepping out in faith when I heard Him tell me to sell, despite not knowing what came next.

We don't have a mountain near us, but we do have Brill Hill. One morning, again at dawn, I got up to go and pray, particularly to give thanks for the abundance of what God had done in our lives. I asked Him why He had given us so much wealth, and I was reminded of the parable of the good steward. A master gave three servants different amounts of money. The one with the least was scared and buried the money in the sand. The one with the most invested wisely and gained interest. The master blessed the servants who invested well and gave them more whilst punishing the one who didn't.

He was telling me that I had been a good steward and so He was trusting me with more. I felt God say, "Those to whom I give much, I expect much," and then three little sheep came into view just in front of Brill Windmill. I heard God speak into my thoughts and say, "Simon, feed My sheep". As I prayed more, I realised that God had given me money to feed people, both spiritually and physically. We now invest the money he has given us into Christian projects such as Bible translation and church planting. We have also set up Challenge Ministries Swaziland in the UK, which raises money to feed, house and educate hundreds of orphaned and vulnerable children in Eswatini.

Sometimes, when God speaks, He wants to reinforce what He has said and will often repeat the same thing another way. Six months later, we were on holiday in Israel as a family. I stood on the beach in Galilee, and there it was on a wooden signpost: "Simon, feed My sheep." Amazing!

Our daughter, Izzy, also had God speak to her supernaturally whilst we were on that holiday in Israel. She was in her mid-teens and had been resisting the pressure from her youth pastor at church to get baptised. We were on the mountain where Jesus preached the sermon on the mount and were singing some worship songs. Apparently, Clare was praying for Izzy at the time, and when we turned around, Izzy was in tears. "What's the matter, darling?" She answered that God had told her it was time to get baptised. A couple of days later, I had the enormous privilege of baptising my daughter in the River Jordan near to where Jesus Himself had been baptised.

We had a tour guide who said she was a Messianic Jew (a Jew who has accepted Jesus as Messiah). This lady said that God had a word of encouragement for Izzy on her baptism day and asked permission to share it. She said that God had given Izzy a gift for children and was going to use her with them later in life.

That same year, we went on a family trip to visit our charity project in Eswatini. We stayed in Bulembu, a town set up as a safe place for orphans to grow up in. The headteacher of the primary school invited us to dinner one evening. She also has a prophetic gifting and regularly has words from God for other people.

Amazingly, she repeated what Karen in Israel had said. God was going to use Izzy to work with children.

Several years later, Izzy chose Early Childhood studies at University and has since worked as a nanny and a teacher in a nursery school.

God also speaks through others He places in our lives for His purposes, and I am so grateful to my discerning Christian friends who have encouraged me with a word from God and a relevant piece of scripture at just the right time.

A few years ago, my parents went on a cruise, and I agreed to drive them to Southampton and pick them up two weeks later. That meant a lot of driving, and I felt I was being a good son, going out of my way for my parents. For their return journey, I had to drive from Oxford to Southampton, pick them up and then drive all the way to Clacton on the Essex coast. On the way I had to fill up with petrol and Mum and Dad had to go to the loo. I locked the car and when I returned, Mum was angry with me for locking her out. I was tired, so reacted in anger. We had a row, and by the time I got to their house, I decided to change my plans. Instead of staying the night, I would drive straight home.

I realised that I was too tired to drive immediately, so decided to go for a walk on the beach to clear my head and my anger. As I walked, my phone pinged, and I received a text from my friend, Pastor Wandi, in Eswatini. I had not heard from him for over a year. The text was a piece of scripture. "Honour your mother and father," it said.

God speaks, and His timing is perfect. I returned to Mum and Dad, made up and stayed the night.

One of the challenges when God speaks into your thoughts is knowing when it is Him and when it is you. When I was a new Christian, I had to learn to discern God speaking from myself speaking. I had invited a non-Christian colleague from work to church, and that night, something weird happened. Someone spoke out in tongues during the praise time. God sometimes gives people the ability to speak in a heavenly language (you can read about that in Acts when the Holy Spirit fell on a crowd of people). The pastor said that sometimes someone else would be given an interpretation of what had been said, so we should pray to see if he would give someone the interpretation.

As we prayed, I felt I knew what God wanted to say. It was about giving your fear to the Lord. In my head, I freaked. Firstly, I thought that there was no way that God would use me as new Christian in this way. Then I thought I was going mad and making it up. Finally, I thought there was no way I would make a fool of myself in front of a work colleague, so I kept my mouth shut.

I could not concentrate or listen to the sermon during the rest of the service. My heart was hammering, and I increasingly felt that God had wanted me to share this thing about giving your fears to Him. After a while, the words "open the Bible" came into my thoughts, so I did and nearly fell off my seat. Some scripture on the page summarised what God had been asking me to share – give your fears to the Lord.

So now I knew that God had spoken and it was not my thoughts. I was scared because I felt like I had to share and do so in front of my colleague. I also realised that I would have to somehow interrupt the service because I had missed my moment earlier. So I prayed, "Lord, I am scared. Please help me share this."

By now, the pastor was playing the last worship song and to my amazement, he stopped playing and said that he felt the Lord wanted him to give another opportunity for the person who didn't share earlier to come forward. I had no choice but to go forward and share what God had been saying.

A couple of years later, I found myself sitting at dinner with this colleague at a sales conference, and she had a little too much to drink. She leaned over and asked me if I remembered when I took her to church. "Yes," I nervously replied, wondering what on earth she was going to say. "That message you shared was for me." Wow! God speaks through us to other people.

Incidents like this have reinforced my belief that God speaks into our thoughts and that we can discern when it is Him rather than ourselves.

A similar incident happened at Abacus. I was interviewing a lady for a senior role in my management team and somehow, at the end of the interview, we talked about her son, who had brittle asthma. He would be normal one moment and then stop breathing the next. She had to revive her son several times and on one occasion, he had died and been brought back in the ambulance. She lived in dread of those catastrophic asthma attacks. I asked if she had faith, and she said, "Yes, in the past, but when I was in crisis with my son, I didn't feel God close to me when I needed Him."

I welled up with tears at her story, as our daughter Amy was the same age as her son. I asked if I could pray for her, and in particular, I asked that God would reveal Himself to her again so she would know for certain that He was there for her.

The interview ended, and I got on with the rest of my day. As I was about to leave in the evening, one of my Christian colleagues, Christie, said that God had given her a piece of scripture, but she had no idea who it was for. Her translation was something like, "Do not dread the day of disaster, for I the Lord am with you." I knew immediately that it was for the lady I had interviewed, as it was the answer to our prayer earlier.

God will use us to speak to others.

God also speaks when we go to church. He will speak through the sermon and through the prayers. He will speak to us as we sing worship songs. He might even speak prophetically to you through someone else at church.

In 2018, I was on another mission trip to Eswatini, and we went to Potters Wheel church in Mbabane for a praise and prayer night. There was no sermon. It was just an evening of worship allowing the Holy Spirit to minister to us. At the time, I was grieving the change in our family life. Amy and Izzy were both at university, so we were now a family of three at home. Adjusting to the empty nest and a change in role as a father is difficult, and I was sad. The worship music set me off, and I found myself weeping, so

I went forward for prayer. I knelt down at the stage, and someone from the prayer team came to pray for me. They didn't ask any questions or talk. I just felt a hand on my shoulder and then these words: "Simon, the Lord is making you a father to many." That person had no idea why I had come forward, but God did. I was comforted by those words, and increasingly, I have seen my role grow, yes, as a father to my three girls but also to the many orphans in Bulembu and the young men and women in our rehabilitation centres. Last year, a young twenty-something whom I have known since she was twelve or so said, "Mr Simon, I never knew my father but I see you as my papa." What a privilege to play the role of father in the lives of many vulnerable young people.

So, let me challenge you. If you don't read the Bible, pray, or go to church, if you don't have any Christian friends, how are you going to hear God's voice? Take this challenge seriously because I can assure you that God really does want to speak to you.

Even we Christians get too busy to find space for God, and we miss out on so much encouragement and direction. Finding time for daily devotion is an excellent discipline, even if it is only five minutes while you eat breakfast. It is remarkable how many times the scripture reading and thought for the day is pertinent to what is happening in your life. I also like to make sure that I pray in the morning for anything I might be facing that day and then throughout the day when the need arises.

I believe in fasting in prayer and meditating on the Word of God. Too often, our prayer life is speaking to God: "Help me with this, heal my friend, get me that job", etc.

The most powerful prayer is "Lord, speak to me," and then sit quietly and wait. If you can find a mountain or a beautiful, quiet place, then even better. Fasting is saying to God, "I want to feed on You", so we replace a meal (or meals) with time with God. In the early days, I made a mistake and just went to work hungry, and that defeated the point. Set aside time with your Bible to see what God has to say.

John 8:47 says, "Whoever belongs to God hears what God says. The reason you do not hear is that you do not belong to God."

As an atheist, I had the arrogance to say to God, "Prove Yourself to me and I will believe." I didn't realise that my very attitude stopped me from hearing from Him.

Once I took that step of faith, He has proved Himself to me over and over again because I hear from Him daily. Occasionally, I feel anxious about something, and if it persists, I eventually realise I am trying to do something in my own strength. At that stage, I stop, pray and ask God to intervene. Sometimes, there will be some unconfessed sin in my life that is preventing me from hearing what He is saying, so I confess and leave it with Jesus. And then I hear from Him and experience that incredible peace that descends when you know you are back in God's will.

God really does speak. We simply have to find the space to listen.

Chapter 6
Are All Religions the Same?
"You shall have no other gods before Me."
– Deuteronomy 5:7

One of my original beliefs was that it didn't matter what religion you followed. They were all vaguely similar, and as long as what you practised in your religion didn't hurt anyone, that was fine.

We live in a culture that doesn't believe in "absolute truth". There is no definitive right or wrong: what is important is what you personally believe. Neither do we like to be told that we are wrong and the idea of saying one religion is right and the others are not, is seen as arrogant and insulting.

So, let me try to unpack this tricky subject.

The table below shows the major world religions and the population size that claim that religion as their own. I have also added whether they are atheistic (do not believe in a god), monotheistic (belief in one god) or polytheistic (belief in lots of gods).

Religion	Estimated global population 2020	What Do They Believe In?
Christianity	2.38 billion	One God (Father, Son, Spirit)
Islam	1.91 billion	One God (Allah)
Judaism	14.6 million	One God (Yahweh)
Hinduism	1.16 billion	Multiple Gods
Folk religions	430 million	Multiple Gods
Buddhism	507 million	No God
Unaffiliated/ atheism	1.19 billion	No God
Other religions	61 million	-

Can all these belief systems be correct? The answer is no. There is either no god, one god, or many gods. Many people in the world, therefore, believe something false.

The question is, does it matter what you believe? Does it matter whether you are right or wrong regarding religion? The Bible says "yes, it does matter" because what you decide to believe during life will impact what happens to you after you die and into eternity. It is so important that God said in the first of the Ten Commandments, "You shall have no other gods before Me."

So any religion that is worshipping multiple gods – things made of stone or precious metals, statues or idols of any kind – is breaking God's commands and will ultimately incur His wrath. Idolatry of any kind is seen as a terrible wickedness in the Bible. The Egyptians worshipped many gods, and when the Jewish nation escaped, they were left in the desert wilderness for a whole generation (about forty years) before entering the promised land. This was all because they had turned away from God to worship the things they had learned about whilst slaves in Egypt. They had made an image of a golden calf to worship and God punished them for it (Exodus 32). If you are praying to anyone or anything that is not God, then you are angering Him and risking His wrath and your future eternity. What you believe and practice really does matter.

All religions try to do two things. Firstly, they create a moral code for living, and secondly, they determine how you relate to the supernatural world, and that influences what happens to you when you die. Jesus summed this up simply. He said, "'Love the Lord your God with all your heart and with all your soul and with all your mind.' This is the first and greatest commandment. And the second is like it: 'Love your neighbour as yourself'" (Matthew 22:37–39).

It is the moral teaching that is often common to all religions, isn't it? A Buddhist, a Christian, a Muslim, a Jew and a Hindu will all be taught about being good and living at peace with one's neighbour. This a healthy message for us to share with one another. We want a world that is at peace and in harmony with one another, don't we?

In fact, it is sad that so many wars and problems between mankind are done in the name of religion. Religious fundamentalists are at the heart of terrorism today, and it is not just the Islamic fundamentalists in the Middle East. We have a war between Jews and Palestinians in Israel. We have atrocities committed in Nigeria and other parts of Africa between Christians and Muslims.

In the past, the Jews have been persecuted, and there is still antisemitism today. In the Middle Ages, we also saw Christians burning people at the stake for the flimsiest of reasons. All done in the name of God.

My old self would have blamed God and religion for these atrocities. My Christian self sees the sin in mankind. It is man who creates these different religions and man who commits these crimes against humanity. Just because they are done in the name of God does not mean that they are of God.

I also believe in Satan, the source of all evil. Much of what we see in the world is a spiritual battle between the forces of good and evil in the spiritual realms. Satan causes division and strife, and one of his main aims is to keep us from knowing God.

Let's consider the key differences between the different belief systems. Since we have already explored the arguments surrounding whether there is a God, I will ignore them in this chapter.

Buddhists do not believe in a supreme God or deity. Instead they believe that human life is one of suffering. Meditation, spiritual and physical labour, and good behaviour are the ways to achieve enlightenment or "nirvana". The path to enlightenment is through the practice and development of morality, meditation and wisdom. Life is both endless and subject to impermanence, suffering and uncertainty.

Hindus believe that life is a series of reincarnations, and what you become in the next life depends on how good you have been in this life. They believe that each individual creates their own destiny by their thoughts, words and deeds (Karma).

Christians, Muslims and Jews believe in one life and Heaven and Hell after one death. Again, what happens after you die depends on what you do in this life. To the Muslim, there is a weighing scale of good and bad. If you do more good than bad, you will go to paradise. To the Jew, you have to be obedient to a myriad of laws in order to get to Heaven – the disobedient go to Hell.

I am a Christian, and we believe that going to Heaven is not based on what we have done; it is determined by what Jesus has already done. His death on the cross paid the penalty for my wrongdoings (sins) and therefore, I am assured of my place in Heaven. We accept that we can never be without sin, so we need Jesus to wash us clean by forgiving us. Once we have done so, we are made perfect for Heaven.

The critical difference between Christianity and all the other religions is that what happens to us when we die is based upon what Jesus, our Saviour, has done for us. It is not based on how good or obedient we are in this life.

Ultimately, it all comes down to Jesus and the resurrection. Was Jesus the Son of God, and does He really have the power over life and death, for Himself and for us? Abraham, Moses, Muhammad and Buddha were all men who died. They didn't claim to be God and they didn't claim to be the judge at the end of time who will decide what happens to us after we die.

So, did Jesus rise from the dead? If He did, then we should believe everything He taught. If He didn't, then it doesn't matter what we believe or what religion we follow because all that counts is how we behave.

There are different theories about the resurrection:

1. The Romans or Jews stole the body of Jesus,

2. The whole story was simply a legend that grew over time,

3. Jesus didn't die on the cross. He fainted and revived later in the tomb,

4. Jesus died, and the disciples simply claimed He had risen again,

5. Visions of Jesus after His death were hallucinations,

6. Jesus died and rose to life three days later.

The first option doesn't work. If the Roman or Jewish authorities had removed Jesus' body, they would have simply revealed the hidden body to dispute whether Jesus had risen, and this would have quashed the idea that He was the Messiah.

We have discussed the accuracy and quality of the historical evidence in chapter two. Jesus was a real person and there are too many ancient documents of testimony to suggest that the resurrection of Jesus was a legend that grew over time. Option two does not work.

Let's take the swoon or coma theory. The Romans were experts at killing people through this horrible process of nailing people through hands and ankles to a cross. John (His best friend) was an eyewitness, and he says that one of the soldiers pierced Jesus' side with a spear, and a sudden flow of blood and water came out (John 19:34). When we die, our plasma separates from our blood cells, and this is a good confirmation that Jesus was dead.

We know that Jesus was embalmed by two people and wrapped in linen cloths (John 19:39–42) and then left in a new tomb with a heavy stone rolled in front of it. Two Roman soldiers were left to guard the tomb to make sure that Jesus' body was not stolen.

So Jesus had seven to nine inch nails in His hands and feet, had been speared in the side and was then placed in a tomb with a stone four to six feet in diameter weighing several hundred kilos. Do you think it plausible that He awoke from a coma and pushed that stone away?

This theory does not stack up. Jesus really did die.

The fourth theory was promoted initially by Jewish religious leaders and is still believed by Muslims, Jews and other groups today. The disciples stole the body and then made up the whole story of the resurrection. First, there is the issue of the Roman soldiers guarding the tomb. The Pharisees had heard about Jesus' prophecy that He would rise after death, so they got the Romans to post guards. They did not want Jesus to fulfil the prophecies about the Messiah.

The disciple Matthew wrote all about what happened on resurrection day (Matthew 28). There was an earthquake, and an angel rolled the stone away. Jesus came out. His appearance was like lightning, and His clothes were as white as snow. We are told that the guards were so afraid that they shook and fell into a faint. Eventually, the guards had to make a report to the chief priests and explain what they saw. They were given a large sum of money and told to claim that the disciples came during the night and stole the body away whilst the guards were asleep. This is the source of that theory.

When I read the Gospel accounts, I see a massive change in the disciples after resurrection day. They were defeated after the crucifixion. They had run away and returned to their everyday lives. After they saw Jesus alive, there was a totally new dynamic. They left their businesses and spent the rest of their lives telling the story of Jesus and what they had observed, including His miracles and the final fulfilment of the Messiah's prophecies about His rising from the dead. Many of the disciples were executed themselves later in life. Do you think anyone would sacrifice everything, including their lives, for a lie? It doesn't stack up; someone would have denounced the lie eventually, particularly when facing their own torture and death.

So, what about the theory of hallucination? It is possible in extreme grief that someone might imagine they are seeing their loved one speaking to them. The problem is that usually, a hallucination happens to one person. We are told in the Bible that Jesus appeared to over five hundred people at one time (1 Corinthians 15:6).

It is highly improbable that the same hallucination happened to so many people all at once.

So I believe, along with billions of other people in history, that Jesus really did die and rise again three days later.

The first person to believe was a Roman soldier before the resurrection. He was present at the execution and saw at the point of Jesus' death some weird things happen. There was an earthquake, tombs broke open and the bodies of many holy people who had died were raised to life, and they were seen by many in Jerusalem. He was terrified and said, "Surely this was the son of God" (Matthew 27:54).

Jesus was seen by so many people and His body was real and physical. It had holes where the nails had been and where the spear had pierced His side. Thomas felt His wounds (John 20:27), Jesus ate fish with His friends (Luke 24:41–43) and Mary Magdalene clung to Him (John 20:17).

The evidence and first-hand accounts all suggest that the resurrection actually happened and that is why Christianity is different from all other religions. Jesus has demonstrated His power over death not just through His own resurrection but those of others. He said that He was the only way to the Father – the only way to Heaven. If there were any other way to save people from death, any other way for people to gain entry to Heaven, then the Son of God would not have needed to endure the agony of crucifixion. If following the Jewish laws was the passport to Heaven, Jesus would not have needed to die. If adhering to any other type of religious belief was enough, then Jesus would not have had to die. But He did.

Jesus had the wisdom to defend Himself against the lies spoken at His trial, yet He remained silent. He had the supernatural power to strike down all the Roman soldiers, but He chose to die. The Son of God had to die and be resurrected to pave the way for you and me, if we accept Him as Saviour, to gain entrance to Heaven. No other religious leader has ever done what Jesus did, and you cannot buy your way into Heaven through your good behaviour and adherence to set religious processes and ceremonies. It all comes down to the resurrection of Jesus.

So, challenge yourself. Do you believe that Jesus was the Son of God who has the power to forgive and who died and rose again so that we may inherit eternal life through Him? It's a really important question that you need an answer to.

I want to touch on one other set of belief systems in this chapter: astrology and the occult.

When I was an atheist, I used to read my daily horoscope and believed that there are twelve different character types based on the month you were born in. I also believed that in relationships, you are more compatible with people of certain star signs than others. I also used to read Chinese horoscopes.

Now, I know that any form of superstition is detestable to the Lord and that there is great spiritual danger in messing with the occult.

Deuteronomy 18 says, "When you enter the land the Lord your God is giving you, do not learn to imitate the detestable ways of the nations there. Let no one be found among you who sacrifices their son or daughter in the fire, who practices divination or sorcery, interprets omens, engages in witchcraft, or casts spells, or who is a medium or spiritist or who consults the dead. Anyone who does these things is detestable to the Lord."

And Leviticus 20:6 says,

"I will set My face against anyone who turns to mediums and spiritists to prostitute themselves by following them, and I will cut them off from their people."

Isaiah 47 talks about astrologers who will be burned in the fire like stubble.

Throughout the Bible, astrologers, mediums and spiritists are all enemies of God, and the people who consult them are doing evil in God's eyes. God sent prophets to warn against them and the consequence of following such evil is death.

The Bible says that God placed the sun, moon and stars to mark time and seasons and provide light. He did not place them to guide and instruct our lives or determine our destiny. That is His job.

God made us each unique. He knew our unformed bodies whilst we were in our mother's wombs. He watches over our lives when we wake and when we go to bed (Psalm 139). He determines the number of days we live (Job 14:5).

Astrology is a form of idolatry, as we are taking our guidance from something other than God. How foolish I was to put my trust in a created thing rather than the Creator Himself. Since realising this, God has been my sole guiding light for thirty years. If you still consult astrology to guide you today, you need to repent and ask Jesus for guidance instead.

Witchcraft and any occult practice is even more dangerous. God forbids you to consult the dead and when you think you are speaking to a loved one, you are being deceived. The Bible talks about God and Satan, angels and demons. I believe what the Bible says, particularly as Jesus Himself taught about these spiritual beings. We are told that Satan set himself against God and was thrown out of Heaven along with fallen angels, whom we now call demons (Revelation 12:7). They can know things about us supernaturally, and they can influence our thinking, behaviours and emotions. In the same way that we can invite Jesus and the Holy Spirit to live in our hearts, we can also invite in Satan and his demons. If you'd attend a séance, you will ask, "Is there anyone out there?" You are inviting in demons, not the spirit of a loved one.

This sounds like science fiction or fantasy, but Jesus Himself took it seriously. He said this:

"When an impure spirit comes out of a person, it goes through arid places seeking rest and does not find it. Then it says, 'I will return to the house I left.' When it arrives, it finds the house swept clean and put in order.

Then it goes and takes seven other spirits more wicked than itself, and they go in and live there. And the final condition of that person is worse than the first" (Luke 11:24–26).

It is possible to become infected with demons and Jesus regularly drove demons out through prayer. These demons impacted people's mental and physical health. They made people violent and evil. They still do today.

I believe that Hitler dabbled with the occult, and his hatred of the Jews stemmed from a satanic influence.

I regularly visit Africa with my charity. Black magic, ancestor worship and all sorts of occult practices through witch doctors are prevalent. Satanic power is real and dangerous.

I was once warned that we were visiting a spiritually dark village and to pray because sometimes Satan would have a go at us through our families. That evening, I got a phone call from home. My daughter Izzy was terrified as she could see snakes in her bedroom. The snake or serpent is a common manifestation of Satan and is at the heart of occult practices in Africa. I prayed for them to go in the name of Jesus, and then Izzy was able to sleep.

On another occasion, my wife Clare and I were introduced to a young man. He had grown up for twenty years tied to a tree because his village described him as demon-possessed and violent as a consequence. He was a living example of the kinds of demon-possessed people that you read about in the Bible. An evangelist through our charity visited his village and prayed for the demons to go, again in the mighty name of Jesus. They left, and the boys' violence disappeared. He now works for a medical charity in Eswatini.

Demons are not just confined to Africa. A pastor friend of mine in the UK had a lady visit as she wanted to leave the witch's coven that she had been a member of. As my friends prayed for the demons to be gone in Jesus' name, she fell to the floor and multiple voices came shrieking out of her.

Clare once woke up in the middle of the night and felt an evil presence in the room. She was terrified and so prayed for protection. She is the only person I know who has seen angels. After she prayed, there was one standing at each corner of our bed. Then, a great peace fell upon her, and she was able to fall asleep. The demons had fled away from the presence of the angels.

I cannot stress this strongly enough: Do not get involved with astrology or the occult. If you have, then the good news is that all spiritual beings have to obey the name of Jesus and so when we pray, we can be cleansed of any satanic influence.

So, to conclude this chapter, most religions focus on being good and that is helpful when we consider our relationships with one another.

The differences between the religions are about how you relate to God and how you get to Heaven. Can you earn your way to Heaven by being good or religiously pious? Christianity says "no" and we are going to consider this further in the next chapter.

Chapter 7
Am I a Good Person?

"If we claim to be without sin, we deceive ourselves, and the truth is not in us."

– 1 John 1:8

I used to think that I was a good person and that if there was a god, he would look upon me favourably.

I have never murdered anyone, and I am pretty honest; in fact, I hate deceit and lying. I give to charity and have helped little old ladies across the road and onto buses. Once, an old lady who was worried about finding the right train, asked me for assistance. So I helped her board the last carriage and walked off feeling proud of myself for being so helpful. Then, to my horror, the front part of her train departed, leaving her behind! That was just an accident, and usually, I am nice. I like to help people.

As a non-believer, I was vaguely aware of the Ten Commandments as a yardstick for knowing right from wrong, and I assumed that I obeyed them. I would have described myself as a good person.

To me, people like Hitler and Saddam Hussein were evil people, and I was more towards the Mother Teresa end of the scale; maybe not quite as good as her, but certainly not evil.

However, now that I am a Christian and have read the Bible, I realise that, like everyone, I am a sinner. It's a word we don't like to use or be accused of, and yet it is a really important word. Sin is the reason we do not hear from or experience God, and sin is the reason we cannot enter Heaven after we die.

Imagine Heaven as a perfect place; somewhere without sin and where God is. Heaven would not remain perfect if any sin is let in, so only perfect people can go there. This leaves us with a problem: none of us are perfect and none of us are without sin. So left on our own, none of us would get to Heaven.

Let's consider sin. Fundamentally, it is putting ourselves, rather than God, at the centre of the universe. It is a state of being where I believe that I am more important than anyone else. My opinion is more important than yours. My needs come first. I will decide what is right or wrong and I don't need God or anyone else telling me what to do. That is the attitude of sin and all other sins come from this.

I steal because I want what you have got. I argue because I'm right and you're wrong. I shout because I want my way. I commit adultery because I am putting my sexual needs before my commitment to my spouse. I get upset when I am overlooked for a promotion at work because I think that I am better than the person who got the job. I lie because I am afraid of the consequences of being found out.

I was shocked when I read the Ten Commandments. I was breaking the first four as a start because they are all about our relationship with God. Jesus described these as the most important of the commandments because who we are and how we think and behave is absolutely determined by our relationship with God.

I was a blasphemer. I didn't swear much, but I used "Jesus" as a mild expletive.

The first thing that happened to me after I asked Jesus to be my Lord was that the blasphemy stopped. Now, I am really sensitive to it in others and I cringe when I hear people taking my Lord's name in vain. They are using the name of the Creator of the universe as a swear word and one day will have to stand before that very Jesus to give an account of themselves.

My idea of being good in God's eyes fell at the first hurdle. By rejecting Him and putting my trust in myself, astrology, or other things to guide me, I was failing the first commandment. By not going to church and not treating the Sabbath as a Holy day, I was failing another commandment. By blaspheming, I was offending God.

At least I was doing well with the last six commandments, which concern how we relate to others (our neighbours).

And then I read Jesus' words in the book of Matthew. When I look at someone lustfully, I am committing adultery in my heart. When I am angry with someone, I am committing murder in my heart.

The threshold for sin is very low from God's perspective, and I have come to the solid conclusion that I am definitely a sinner, just like the rest of humanity.-

And what is the consequence of sin? We are separated from God, and our relationships with one another are ruined. Sin is at the root of all human unhappiness. If we perfectly trusted God to provide, we would not be anxious. If we truly believed in eternal life after we die, then not even death would phase us. Wars, poverty, global warming and the pollution of our planet are all caused by man's sin.

A Holy God casts the death penalty. No sin is allowed in Heaven, so how on earth can any of us get there? Certainly not on our own merits.

It doesn't matter how much money we give away to charity or how many old ladies we help onto the train. We can say nice things to people and not swear, but we are still imperfect before God and unworthy of a place in a perfect Heaven.

Interestingly, even our religious practices are not enough.

Isaiah 1:13 says, "Stop bringing meaningless offerings! Your incense is detestable to Me. New Moons, Sabbaths and convocations – I cannot bear your worthless assemblies."

In Matthew 23, Jesus condemns the Jewish religious leaders. He calls them hypocrites who like to be seen as righteous but, on the inside, are wicked.

"Woe to you, teachers of the law and Pharisees, you hypocrites! You are like whitewashed tombs, which look beautiful on the outside but on the inside are full of the bones of the dead and everything unclean. In the same way, on the outside, you appear to people as righteous, but on the inside, you are full of hypocrisy and wickedness" (Matthew 23:27).

These religious leaders looked down on everyone else and were constantly condemning others for not obeying the religious laws perfectly. Everything they did was for others to see their self-righteousness.

Jesus said that these religious hypocrites were closing the door to Heaven for themselves and for those that they taught.

"Woe to you, teachers of the law and Pharisees, you hypocrites! You shut the door of the kingdom of Heaven in people's faces. You yourselves do not enter, nor will you let those enter who are trying to" (Matthew 23:14).

Have a read of Matthew 23 if you want to hear all of Jesus' words on this topic. Basically, He taught that perfect religious obedience does not buy your way to Heaven and that is why any religion that teaches that you have to be a good person is missing the point.

I used to think that churchgoers were self-righteous people who looked down on the rest of us "sinners" with judgment and disdain.

I have learned that the opposite is true. I was being self-righteous when I declared myself a good person. Righteousness is being right before God, and I declared myself right before Him without having ever considered what it meant. The people I meet in church are people who have recognised themselves as sinners unworthy of God and unworthy of a place in Heaven.

The reason for the Ten Commandments and religious law is to act as a mirror. When we hold our lives up to God's Word (the Bible), we see that we all fall short of what He wants for us. We see our sin, and therefore, we see a need to do something about it. We realise that we need to be forgiven and we need to be washed clean for Heaven.

That is the good news message of Christianity. None of us can be perfect, none of us can be good enough for Heaven, and so Jesus, the Son of God, gives us a free pass. He is the one who forgives us when we turn to Him and ask forgiveness (repent). He is the One who has paid the death penalty on our behalf. He alone is the One who has the authority and the power to cleanse us of anything and make us perfect in the eyes of God the Father.

Interestingly, Jesus spent most of His time with sinners – people the religious leaders would not go near to. Take a prostitute, a murderer or an addict whose lives have been unimaginable: They see the dirt of their lives and the size of their sin and are therefore so much more grateful to be forgiven. They are often so amazed to find that they are accepted by God despite what they have done.

That is the problem with us "good" people. We are blind to our sins and our rejection of God and, therefore, do not see a need to repent and ask to be forgiven by Jesus. Unless we do that, there is nothing else we can do to be made fit for Heaven once we die.

Dealing with your sin really is a life-or-death decision. I spoke earlier in Chapter Four of the need to be born again. This process is simple, and we do not need a degree in theology to be ready for Heaven. We have to recognise that we are not "good" people and that, in many ways, we have rejected God and refused to obey His commands. We have to ask Jesus to forgive us, accept that He paid the death penalty for us and then be filled with the Holy Spirit. Then, we are born again and made spiritually ready for life in Heaven once we die.

Now, here is a hard thing. God calls us to live Holy lives. That means living lives that are distinct from society: we are to be set apart as His Holy people. That means not conforming to the ways of the world.

The apostle Paul describes what life filled with the Holy Spirit should look like compared to our previous lives.

"You, my brothers and sisters, were called to be free. But do not use your freedom to indulge the flesh; rather, serve one another humbly in love. For the entire law is fulfilled in keeping this one command: 'Love your neighbour as yourself.' If you bite and devour each other, watch out or you will be destroyed by each other.

So I say, walk by the Spirit, and you will not gratify the desires of the flesh. For the flesh desires what is contrary to the Spirit, and the Spirit what is contrary to the flesh. They are in conflict with each other, so that you are not to do whatever you want. But if you are led by the Spirit, you are not under the law.

The acts of the flesh are obvious: sexual immorality, impurity and debauchery; idolatry and witchcraft; hatred, discord, jealousy, fits of rage, selfish ambition, dissensions, factions and envy; drunkenness, orgies, and the like. I warn you, as I did before, that those who live like this will not inherit the kingdom of God.

But the fruit of the Spirit is love, joy, peace, forbearance, kindness, goodness, faithfulness, gentleness and self-control. Against such things there is no law. Those who belong to Christ Jesus have crucified the flesh with its passions and desires. Since we live by the Spirit, let us keep in step with the Spirit. Let us not become conceited, provoking and envying each other." – Galatians 5:13–26

Jesus wants to change us from the inside out. He wants to change us into the people we should be and is interested in our hearts and characters. He changes how we think, feel and behave – not through religious obedience and discipline but through desire and love.

The scripture above shows that there is a conflict between our natural desires and behaviours and the ones we should express when filled with the Holy Spirit. As a Christian, I am a forgiven sinner, and I still sin. I still get angry sometimes. I can easily get offended and have arguments with others. I can still be lustful or desire things I don't yet have. I can be proud or self-reliant at times.

But I do think that God has been chipping away at me over the last thirty years, making me a better version of myself.

I still have my logical, scientific brain. I have the same sense of humour. I still enjoy people, parties, good wine and music. The basics of who I was are still there, including some of my flaws.

But I do like to think that I am less arrogant, gentler and more humble. My questions are now seeking more of God rather than trying to find objections. God has changed personal ambition and materialism into a desire to please Him and towards generosity. I am filled with thankfulness as I realise that everything comes from Him, and He has blessed me abundantly.

I used to be utterly self-reliant and prided myself on being strong and capable. Now, I rely upon Him for everything and see that when I am weak, God is strong in my life. That's usually when the best outcome happens because I am doing something in His will, not mine. I said earlier that the blasphemy was erased from my vocabulary as soon as I asked Jesus to be my Lord. I have become very sensitive and compassionate to the needs of others and cry easily.

I also care deeply about sharing the good news that Jesus brought, and God has given me many opportunities to speak with all sorts of people over the last thirty years. We don't evangelise because we want to win an intellectual argument. We share because we want to see those that we love saved from death. I hate to see needless anxiety and unhappiness and get frustrated when people choose to suffer when I have experienced the peace that comes through prayer and trusting God for my future.

How would you feel if someone you love was a smoker and you knew that it was going to give them cancer one day? You share with them over and over again to tell them to stop smoking, not because you are judgemental but because you love them. Then they get cancer, but you have discovered a cure. It will save them from dying. To your horror, they refuse to accept the cure because they don't believe it will work. Imagine the frustration and sadness you would feel, particularly after they die. That is how I feel about sharing with my family and friends. It is sin that is leading to death, and there is a cure, and His name is Jesus.

God has given me a passion and a boldness to share about Jesus with others; this book is part of that. I hope that I do it with gentleness and sensitivity.

My driving force now is my desire to please and obey my Heavenly Father. I want to be holy not because I am told I should be, but because I want to be. I go to church not because I am told to, but because I want to. When you allow Jesus and the Holy Spirit in, it is all about desire, not duty.

Going to church is not what makes you a Christian, but I don't believe that you can be without going (unless you physically can't). That sounds contradictory, doesn't it? The act of going to church or being religious is not what saves you. That is purely down to being forgiven by Jesus.

However, when you are born again and filled with the Holy Spirit, you start to express the fruit of God in your life, and one of those is that you desire to go to church. I love being in fellowship with other Christians. I love praising God through music and hearing Him speak through a sermon. I believe God created music so we can connect with Him spiritually. It does something to our emotions and when we are praising, our spirits connect with His, and we find ourselves more in tune with Him and more able to hear what He is saying.

I am also grateful to my mid-week life group. We pray together, grow together, encourage one another, cry and laugh together. God wants us to be in community; without church, our faith shrivels. A sign of being born again is that you will desire to be with other Christians praising God.

To conclude this chapter, I realise I am not a good person. I need God in my life; I need Jesus to keep forgiving me when I mess up, and slowly, since 1991, He has been changing me from the inside out. My heart's desires and priorities are different from thirty years ago. I am a work in progress and there are still many edges that need to be knocked off. However, I do know that my future after I die is assured, and one day, I will be made perfect and fit for Heaven.

Do you still think that you are a good person? I hope not.

SIMON HOWARD

Chapter 8
Facing Uncertainty with Confidence

*"'For I know the plans I have for you,' declares the Lord,
'Plans to prosper you and not to harm you, plans to give
you hope and a future.'"*

– Jeremiah 29:11

I know lots of people who are anxious and fearful of life. We have lived through the COVID pandemic, where many people died globally. There is currently a cost of living crisis, and many are struggling to pay bills as inflation has been at record levels. Multiple wars are happening around the world. There seems to be good reason to be fearful and several of us have stopped watching the news.

Anxiety is nearly always attached to future uncertainty. Will I be able to pay the bills tomorrow? Am I in danger of being made redundant? Will my loved one survive this health scare? Will I get the grades I need to go to university? How am I going to solve this problem at work?

I used to be totally self-reliant. It was something I saw as a strength, yet I have learned as a Christian that my greatest weakness is self-reliance. When I try to do something through my own grit and determination, I often fail and struggle emotionally. When I let go and accept that I can't cope on my own, God's strength kicks in and anxiety is replaced by peace.

Relying upon God rather than myself was a tough lesson, and I think I learned it the hard way. Let me tell you the story of Abacus International.

I shared earlier that I met Andy Duggan at Searle Pharmaceuticals and through him, I became a Christian. He set up a health economic consultancy company called Abacus International and I left my safe job in pharmaceutical marketing to join him as Director about eighteen months later. We helped the medical industries develop and communicate cost-effectiveness arguments to support the launch and marketing of their products. Abacus developed Excel spreadsheet models to demonstrate the impact of new drugs and medical devices in the market. When the UK government established the National Institute for Clinical Excellence (NICE), we were involved in pioneering the process of Health Technology Assessments (HTA). Being the first company in the world to be doing this kind of work was really exciting.

I worked from home in Thatcham near Newbury and commuted to the office in Bicester about once a week. I loved the lifestyle, working from home, visiting clients in the South-East whenever needed and being at the forefront of this new discipline called health economics. Our first two daughters, Amy and then Izzy, came along during this time and I appreciated the flexibility of working from home. When there was a nativity, sports day, or any other family commitment, I could fit work around it. The girls became settled and happy in preschool and then primary and we were very happy as a family at Bucklebury church. These were idyllic times.

After five years, Abacus celebrated making its first one million pounds in revenue. We started investing in more staff to gear up for growth because people are the product of a consultancy. You are selling their skills and time. Unfortunately, revenues stayed at the one million pound level while our costs grew exponentially due to the increase in salaries.

And then came the event that changed the course of my life. Andy was killed in a motorbike accident on the A41 between Aylesbury and Bicester. We had celebrated his fiftieth birthday the weekend before by seeing Carmen at the Albert Hall. As we parted that evening, he gave me a bear hug, and the last words he ever spoke to me were, "love you."

The following Saturday, I received the dreaded phone call and initially went into shock. I was just stunned. In church the following day, as I shared what had happened with a couple of friends, tears began to flow as we prayed.

As the shock wore off, I was hit with the enormity of the consequences. Fear came flooding in. What was going to happen at work? Would I have to get a new job? There were fifteen staff at Abacus at the time and some of them had never worked anywhere else. All our livelihoods were on the line and my mortgage was enormous. Clare had given up her work when Amy came along so the family and staff were dependent upon me.

Andy asked me two weeks before the accident if I would consider taking over as CEO. He realised that he loved doing project work for clients but had identified me as someone who could potentially run the business side of things. I said "no", as I didn't feel ready for the size of this responsibility and I enjoyed the freedom of working from home rather than the office.

Fortunately, he made this suggestion at a board meeting in front of the other two directors so that they would know his wishes when we were discussing leadership succession after he died.

It didn't take long to decide what to do after Andy's death. We had a responsibility to the fifteen families to survive. Debbie, Andy's widow, and the other directors agreed that I would become Managing Director and start running the company despite my misgivings about not being ready.

In my first week in the role, we discovered that our cash flow was in a desperate position. Staff salaries had to be paid the next week, and we owed the tax man a hefty sum. We had twenty-five thousand pounds of debt on credit cards and an overdraft facility of twenty-five thousand. I needed to find forty-five thousand pounds that next week in order to pay for everything and Abacus was technically insolvent. We applied to Barclays to extend our overdraft to fifty thousand pounds with the comfort of knowing that Andy had a key man insurance policy that would eventually bring in a few hundred thousand pounds to help us get back on our feet.

In that first week, I had to communicate the shocking news of Andy's death to staff and clients alike and reassure them that Abacus would continue and that jobs and projects were safe.

I had to deal with lawyers about share transfers as none of the directors were shareholders at the time, as well as walk alongside Debbie and her three young sons, who were all grieving. They asked me to deliver the eulogy at Andy's funeral, a massive privilege but also quite a daunting responsibility.

At the end of week one, Barclays not only refused the overdraft extension but also withdrew our existing facility. Welcome to the life of an MD and business owner.

You can imagine the levels of stress I was under. As well as dealing with my own grief and, of course, my existing client project workload, I now had all this extra responsibility. My cosy life in Thatcham was turned upside down as I had to commute to the office daily, over an hour each way. I often cried on my way up to the office and on the way home, but this is where I learned utter dependence upon God. My faith really kicked in just at the time of greatest crisis.

We had several churches praying for our circumstances and for me as I tried to cope with everything coming our way. I can honestly say that I felt a calm strength descend upon me as I entered the office front door every morning. God gave me the ability to see things clearly and the ability to make decisions about all sorts of issues that I had never had to deal with before. In those first weeks, a client sent me a cheque for twenty-five thousand pounds and promised that he would find a project to put against it. HSBC stepped in and gave us the overdraft we needed. Junior staff stepped up and took on Andy's workload in addition to their own. I was forced to delegate responsibility quickly, and everyone pulled together. We wanted to survive.

Andy died on 15 March 2003 and by the end of that month, we had to close the financial year. Revenue had declined to nine hundred and fifty thousand pounds, and we had made a loss of one hundred and ten thousand pounds. Our business plan for the following year showed that just to break even, we needed the greatest growth in sales that Abacus had ever achieved in the absence of Andy, who had brought in over fifty per cent of the prior year's new business. A miracle was needed.

For the next ten years, I learned that whenever I looked forward at our business plan projections, I would gulp at the size of the task. Anxiety could creep in if I let it. However, when I looked back at our financial results every year, I saw God's blessing at work. We didn't break even the year after Andy's death – we made one hundred thousand pounds profit. The following year, two hundred thousand pounds profit, and the year after that, four hundred thousand pounds. This growth continued for ten years, and I remember marvelling at the point when our expenditure rather than revenue was one million. By now I was hearing God say, "Look back to what I have done in the past and trust what I will do in the future."

I was slowly learning to rely upon God rather than myself through these enormous life challenges.

About a month after Andy's death, we were in Torquay for the Easter holidays and visited a church we had never been to before. I was feeling all wrung out, tired and emotional and wondering if I was good enough to do the job I had been thrown into. It had been an exceptionally hard month. During the worship time, a lady spoke out a prophetic word, and we knew immediately that it was for us. It was based upon some scripture in Isaiah and was a wonderful example of how God speaks to encourage us just when we need it.

"Do you not know? Have you not heard? The Lord is the everlasting God, the Creator of the ends of the earth. He will not grow tired or weary, and His understanding no one can fathom. He gives strength to the weary and increases the power of the weak. Even youths grow tired and weary, and young men stumble and fall; but those who hope in the Lord will renew their strength. They will soar on wings like eagles; they will run and not grow weary, they will walk and not be faint" (Isaiah 40:38–41).

During that time, I was also reminded of another prophetic word spoken over me by someone at "New Wine" – a Christian conference that we used to attend as a family. On the last night of a week's celebration, we were in a giant marquee with around five thousand Christians for an evening celebration. A lady sitting behind Clare and I spoke to us at the end of the evening, and she said that God had given her something to share with each of us (Clare, myself and baby Amy) at the beginning of the week. She chickened out and missed her chance, so she prayed that if God wanted her to speak with us, He would make another opportunity happen. Five nights later, she suddenly saw us sitting in front of her again, another example of God-incidences when we pray. I remember her telling me that there was going to be rocky ground ahead, but I was not to worry. He was going to give me the ability to walk smoothly over this bumpy ground.

After the death of Andy a few years later, I realised that this was the period of my life that she had been referring to, and I was comforted when I remembered that God had promised to help me navigate this thorny path of life.

The world sees weakness as a bad thing and inner strength and self-reliance as a good thing. I have learned that this is the opposite of what God thinks. He wants to be in our lives, and it is often during the tough seasons that we are more likely to lean on Him. My faith grew enormously during those difficult early years running Abacus.

There is great comfort in knowing that Jesus has a plan for your life and that He is guiding you and helping you. When even death has a certain future, you can get through anything.

The Bible teaches that God sometimes uses suffering to refine us (Romans 5:3–4). When life is tough, He works in us to shape us and prepare us for something else. He used the experience of running Abacus to make me more reliant upon Him and less reliant on myself.

Looking back, I can also see other times of difficulty when God has done something to change me. In the pain of the moment it can be hard to see it, but on reflection later in life, God often reveals what He was doing.

For example, I bought my first house in 1990 with a 100% mortgage. I became a Christian in 1991 and in the early nineties, the housing market collapsed, and many of us ended up in negative equity. Becoming a Christian didn't protect me from life's everyday challenges, but I believe that God used those financial difficulties to shape me. He wanted to erase materialism from my heart, and I now know that He was preparing me to manage wealth later in life.

My career was doing well, yet the negative equity on the empty house in Norfolk was getting worse and worse. At one point, interest rates went up to about 15%. Searle Pharmaceuticals were paying the rent for my house in Aylesbury as part of a relocation package, and I was stuck with a ridiculous mortgage on a house that I couldn't sell and which was losing value every month. Financial worries really can take a toll.

After several years of this burden, I attended an evening service at church. The sermon was all about money, based on a scripture saying that it is easier for a camel to go through the eye of a needle than for a rich man to enter Heaven. Being rich is not the problem. Loving money and chasing after it is. That night, I felt God take an emotional burden that had been there for years off my shoulders. I felt Him say that He was going to remove my financial problems as I had at last learned from the lessons of the past years.

The very next morning my boss, John, came into my office and said, "We need to talk about your relocation package. It's gone on far too long." Initially, I panicked, thinking that I would not be able to afford both my mortgage on my Norfolk house and my rent in Aylesbury.

Searle had been paying my rent for three years when I moved to Knutsford and then later to Aylesbury. It was exceptionally generous, as was John's offer to me. If I signed an agreement to stay working for Searle for the next three years, they would take my house in Norfolk and give it to their property agents, who would sell it at whatever price point was required.

God was amazing in how He honoured what He had said the night before. The property was sold at a sixteen thousand pound loss, which thirty years ago was a lot of money. Searle paid twelve thousand pounds of the loss, and I was left to pay four thousand, which happened to be exactly what I had in savings. Isn't God good!

God took away my debt and my savings at the same time. He was saying, "Trust in Me to provide."

I do think I needed that period of financial difficulty for God to challenge attitudes of materialism in me, and so now, when I face hardship, I try to look at the circumstances and ask, "What is God trying to do through this difficulty?"

The Bible is full of messages about trusting God rather than living in fear and anxiety. We have seen that nearly all anxiety is linked to some form of uncertainty in our lives, and so if we learn to trust that God has our futures in His hands, then anxiety subsides.

Whenever I am feeling stressed or worried about something, I eventually look at myself and think, "What am I not trusting God with this time?" I then try to hand it over to Him in prayer.

One of my favourite scriptures is in Philippians:

"Do not be anxious about anything, but in every situation, by prayer and petition, with thanksgiving, present your requests to God. And the peace of God, which transcends all understanding, will guard your hearts and your minds in Christ Jesus" (Philippians 4:6–7).

It is an amazing truth that when you switch from focusing your thoughts on the cause of your worry and lift your eyes to God, He fills you with supernatural peace. We are told to pray with thanksgiving. Do you know that God has hard-wired a chemical reaction into our bodies so that when we give thanks, endorphins are released and we feel better?

I know what it feels like to be awake at night worrying about something. All you want to do is go to sleep, and yet the same nagging thought goes round and round your head. It's horrible! The answer is to think about things in your life that you have to be grateful for and then pray and give thanks to God for them. You will find that He will fill you with a peace that defies your circumstances. That peace guards your heart and your mind, i.e., your thought life can settle, and ultimately, you can sleep.

I am so grateful for the amazing things God has done in my life so far and for the fact that I know He holds my future in His hands. I pray that if you are going through specific challenges right now, you will learn to ask Jesus to fill you with His Spirit and with His peace that passes all understanding.

Trust Him and sleep well!

Chapter 9
Is Death the Final Frontier?

"But unless you repent, you too will all perish."

– Luke 13:3

Death is probably the event we are most scared of and yet it is the one certainty in life. We are all going to die at some point. When I was a child, my greatest fear was the thought of my parents dying. My dad used to commute to London during the time of the troubles in Ireland, and the IRA would sometimes cause bomb scares. I remember being afraid several times because he was late getting home, and it was in the time before mobile phones, so we couldn't find out where he was.

Now, as a father myself, my concern would shift to my children. Once, one of my daughters had to have a brain scan. The drive to get the results was full of terrible anxiety, a sickening fear of hearing bad news.

So, if death is the worst thing we have to face, why do we find it so hard to talk about it? Why do we not consider religion and what it has to say about death and what happens next?

Many people console themselves when someone they love has died with a platitude that they have gone to Heaven. They do this out of blind faith and hope, whether or not they have any religious beliefs. Many people assume that everyone goes to Heaven and that our loved ones are now somewhere up there looking down upon us. That is not what the Bible teaches.

I am going to be deliberately plain-speaking and provocative in this chapter, but I do not want to cause hurt or offence. My motive is for you to take seriously a decision that I believe will impact what happens to you when you die. I want you to fully understand the seriousness of Hell and eternity.

Imagine a pair of unborn twins in the womb. One believes that soon they will pass into another world: one of air and light and sound and smell and touch. A wonderful new adventure.

The other one does not believe. They think the watery life in the dark of the womb is all there is.

In a few days, both these twins will be born. They will cross over into a new realm despite what they believe. It is going to happen, and that is what death is like. You and I will cross over to something else whether we believe that or not.

I will consider three scenarios that could happen at the point of death.

1. There is nothing,

2. We go to Heaven,

3. We go to Hell.

If there is nothing, then none of what I am saying is important. We are just a bunch of bones covered with skin and cartilage; filled with blood and organs. Our thoughts are just electrical impulses and our emotions are governed by hormones and other chemicals. When we die, the elements we are made of are recycled and return to the earth. Ashes to ashes and dust to dust. That's it!

When I first spoke with Andy at Searle, this was what I thought, and it is a sad belief, isn't it? The end! Finished! Nothing more! The optimist in me wanted to believe in something else beyond death, and it was that hope that moved my questions from being objections to seeking answers.

I now believe that all of us are both physical and spiritual. Our spirit is the essence of who we are, and our emotions are linked to our spiritual wellbeing. My spirit is the part of me that makes me who I am. It is the part of me that loves my wife and children, that laughs and cries and fears.

When I became a Christian, I invited the Holy Spirit to dwell in me, and when I hear God speak, His Spirit is talking to my spirit. I really do believe that there is a physical world and a spiritual world, which also includes God, angels, Satan and demons.

So, if there is a spiritual realm that we are part of, what happens when we die? The Bible says that we either go to Heaven or Hell.

I mentioned earlier the challenge we all had when Andy, the founder of Abacus International, was killed in a motorbike accident. About a week after his death, Tony, one of the other directors who became my business partner, had a vision. He saw Andy smiling and dancing in Heaven, and it was real enough to him to encourage him to become a Christian.

In that first week, I raged at God. Why did you take this man? He was only fifty years old and had such a godly influence on many people. He was an evangelist who had led many to Christ. He was a brilliant preacher and of course, he was my friend and boss. I was really upset with God.

God spoke to me as I prayed in anger and pain. He showed me Heaven and earth from His perspective. We think of our side of the divide as the land of the living, and when people die, they cross over to the land of death. That is the opposite of reality. We are living in the land of the dying, and God showed me that Andy had crossed over into the land of life.

His Kingdom is a place of love, light and peace. It is a place without sin or evil of any kind. There are no wars, disease, anger or dissension. There is no death and no fear. It is a place of music and celebration, where we join with millions of angels in praise to our God, who is the source of everything that is good. As our relationship with Him is fully restored, He becomes our love, our light and our peace.

God had chosen Andy to cross over to a heavenly party and blessed him by taking him early. Andy never had to suffer old age or face other challenges in later life. His wife and sons, family and friends have all had to suffer grief, but in the perspective of eternity, a few decades is only for a short time. Then, one day, we will be reunited in a place of joy. Like the baby being born into a new life of adventures, we can cross over from death into an eternity of another type of life, and it will be wonderful.

Now, to the hard part. Hell! Jesus Himself spoke a lot about Heaven and Hell, what it is like and who goes where when they die. We need to be frightened of Hell because we need to do something to avoid going there. Remember, this is a place where you could be stuck forever with no escape, devoid of love and outside of a relationship with God.

The most common word used to describe Hell in the Bible is the word "torment". Imagine your worst nightmare. For me, it would be in a place that is hot and claustrophobic. I panic when I am in small spaces and cannot move forward or backwards. Hell will be worse than your greatest fear. It is a place where Satan and the demons will be confined, so it is a place of great evil. It is also a place where God is absent, and He is the source of all love and light. Hell will be dark, and people will be in physical and mental anguish. There will be no love whatsoever because God is love, and He is in Heaven. Instead of heavenly music, there will be the sound of wailing and agony.

Many of us are innately scared of the dark, and I think that is because it gives us a foretaste of Hell.

Revelation 21:8 describes Hell like this:

"But the cowardly, the unbelieving, the vile, the murderers, the sexually immoral, those who practice magic arts, the idolaters and all liars – they will be consigned to the fiery lake of burning sulphur. This is the second death."

Hell is definitely a place to be avoided at all costs.

Jesus told this story to explain Hell:

"There was a rich man who was dressed in purple and fine linen and lived in luxury every day. At his gate was laid a beggar named Lazarus, covered with sores and longing to eat what fell from the rich man's table. Even the dogs came and licked his sores. The time came when the beggar died and the angels carried him to Abraham's side. The rich man also died and was buried. In Hades, where he was in torment, he looked up and saw Abraham far away, with Lazarus by his side. So he called to him, 'Father Abraham, have pity on me and send Lazarus to dip the tip of his finger in water and cool my tongue, because I am in agony in this fire.' But Abraham replied, 'Son, remember that in your lifetime you received your good things, while Lazarus received bad things, but now he is comforted here and you are in agony. And besides all this, between us and you a great chasm has been set in place, so that those who want to go from here to you cannot, nor can anyone cross over from there to us.' He answered, 'Then I beg you, father, send Lazarus to my family, for I have five brothers. Let him warn them, so that they will not also come to this place of torment.' Abraham replied, 'They have Moses and the Prophets; let them listen to them.' 'No, Father Abraham,' he said, 'but if someone from the dead goes to them, they will repent.' He said to him, 'If they do not listen to Moses and the Prophets, they will not be convinced even if someone rises from the dead'" (Luke 16:19–31).

Jesus says that there is a chasm between Heaven and Hell, and once you are in Hell, that's it. Nothing you can do will change your eternal fate, and you will be in agony and torment forever. The fear of this happening to the ones I love spurs me on to share the Gospel with them.

We also read these words of Jesus in Luke 13:

"He said to them, 'Make every effort to enter through the narrow door, because many, I tell you, will try to enter and will not be able to. Once the owner of the house gets up and closes the door, you will stand outside knocking and pleading, 'Sir, open the door for us.' But He will answer, 'I don't know you or where you come from.' Then you will say, 'We ate and drank with you, and you taught in our streets.' But He will reply, 'I don't know you or where you come from. Away from Me, all you evildoers!' There will be weeping there, and gnashing of teeth, when you see Abraham, Isaac and Jacob and all the prophets in the kingdom of God, but you yourselves thrown out. People will come from east and west and north and south and will take their places at the feast in the kingdom of God."

Many of the people Jesus was speaking to were religious leaders. He is saying that the door to Heaven is very narrow. Even your religiousness is not good enough. We talked about being good in the last chapter. You will never be good enough for Heaven and cannot buy your way in through your behaviour. It is a relationship with God that saves, not our good deeds.

The harsh truth is that you and I will not be in Heaven unless we have repented and been born again through faith in Jesus. The only other destiny is Hell. Jesus is the only way (We covered this in the earlier chapter on religions.).

Jesus gave this warning: "I tell you, My friends, do not be afraid of those who kill the body and after that can do no more. But I will show you whom you should fear: Fear Him who, after your body has been killed, has authority to throw you into Hell. Yes, I tell you, fear Him" (Luke 12:4).

We need to fear the righteous anger of Jesus as well as love the gracious forgiveness of Jesus, as He is the one given authority to judge all mankind.

Let's talk about the end of the world and judgement day. It is a shame that people carrying placards on their backs declaring, "The end of the world is nigh", have turned the subject into one of ridicule as, again, it is something we should take seriously.

When I was doing my O-levels, people were talking about an ancient prophecy from some supposed mystic that declared the world was going to end. I half thought that I might not need to revise so hard if the end came before the exams! Of course, it didn't.

Over the years, we have been scared about nuclear annihilation and, more recently,—global warming as possible ways that the world will end.

Jesus gave a very clear account of what happens at the end, which you can read about in Matthew 24.

One day, after a series of escalating global events that we will cover in the next chapter, everything will go dark. The sun, moon and stars will stop shining against all the laws of science, and this will be a scary and supernatural experience. Heavenly bodies will literally be shaken and fall from the sky. Into that darkness will come a light, and it will be Jesus surrounded by millions of angels. Jesus said at that time, all people on the earth will mourn their sin when they see Him in power and glory. This will be a very different arrival from being born as a baby in a stable. There will be loud trumpet calls, and the dead believers will be raised to life to join Him with the angels.

Then, everyone who has ever lived will be judged alongside Satan. You can read about this in Revelation 20:

The Judgment of the Dead

"Then I saw a great white throne and Him who was seated on it. The earth and the heavens fled from His presence, and there was no place for them. And I saw the dead, great and small, standing before the throne, and books were opened. Another book was opened, which is the Book of Life. The dead were judged according to what they had done as recorded in the books. The sea gave up the dead that were in it, and death and Hades gave up the dead that were in them, and each person was judged according to what they had done. Then death and Hades were thrown into the lake of fire. The lake of fire is the second death. Anyone whose name was not found written in the Book of Life was thrown into the lake of fire."

So how will Jesus decide who goes to Hell and who goes to Heaven? We have already said that it is not based on our perfection, as none of us can be good enough for a perfect God. Instead, God's final verdict will be based upon our relationship with Him. Have we accepted Jesus as our Lord and Saviour while we lived?

A few years ago, I went to a ceremony for a friend who wanted to become a British citizen after several years of living in the UK. She had to swear allegiance to the late Queen as part of the process of being accepted into our United Kingdom. Being adopted into the Kingdom of God is precisely the same. We have to swear allegiance to the King, and when we meet Him, He will say, "Welcome, My beloved." If we have rejected Him, He will say, "I never knew you. Away from Me, you evildoers!"

One question I used to ask was this, "What about people who were born before Jesus and people who have never heard about Him? Surely, it would be unjust to send these people to Hell?"

I trust that God is perfectly just, so I think the rules for judgment are different before and after Christ. I believe that Abraham, Moses and the righteous Jewish believers will be in Heaven because they obeyed God's laws. I trust that babies who die in the womb will go to Heaven because God is merciful. They have never had the chance to hear the Gospel of Jesus. Thankfully, it is not we who decide, but a perfectly just Jesus and that gives me comfort.

Those of us who have heard what Jesus preached and have chosen to accept or reject Him will be judged accordingly. Jesus will not return until the last possible person on earth has heard the Gospel message and has had a chance to be saved from eternal torment. It is one of the reasons that Bible translation organisations are working so hard to make the Bible available in all the languages of the earth. Once this work is complete, then, it will pave the way for Jesus' second coming.

If we return to the question of how can a loving God send people to this terrible place called Hell, we have to remember that He is not suddenly putting us there without warning. Over and over again, He has warned mankind for thousands of years about Hell and the consequences of rejecting Him and carrying on with our sinful lives. Jesus has opened the door to Heaven by what He did on the cross and asks us to walk through that door by coming to Him. If we choose not to, then that is our fault, not His. We, by default, are choosing Hell by ignoring the warnings.

One other thing I have learned as a Christian: Heaven is not some ethereal, spiritual place, and we won't be floating around on clouds with God. In the beginning, God walked with man in the Garden of Eden here on earth. He is going to restore that relationship, and the description at the end of time is one of Jesus coming down to a renewed earth to rule. God restores a new Heaven and a new earth and lives here with us. We are given new resurrection bodies to live on earth in a physical sense. We can get a glimpse of what a resurrection body is like because Jesus was seen post-death in His resurrection body by hundreds of people. We will talk, sing, eat, touch, smell, and see and recognise one another. With all that celebration and music going on, I hope there is a need for pianists, and because it is perfect, I will never hit a wrong note ever again.

This is such a lovely picture that gives amazing hope to those of us who believe. My body aches after a bit of exercise, and I am starting to feel the impact of ageing. My mum has lost her sight, cannot walk and has dementia. It is sad to see the ageing process, but that is countered by the hope I get from my faith. One day, my mum, who believes in Jesus, will be raised from the dead, and she will be given a perfect new body that will never age. She will be able to dance again, ride a bike and skip if she wants to, and I can't wait to see her like that again.

In summary, I used to be scared of death, and now, as a Christian, I am looking forward to being with my Lord and my loved ones in Heaven. My fear is simply for the ones I care about in life who have rejected Jesus as their Saviour and who, therefore, face an eternity in Hell. I will not stop witnessing to them and praying for them until it is too late, i.e. when they or I die.

Chapter 10
The World Through God's Eyes
"Blessed are the meek, for they will inherit the earth."
– Matthew 5:5

The world is a very dark place right now, and – as previously mentioned – many people live in fear and anxiety. It is estimated that over six million people died during the COVID-19 pandemic in recent years.[10] In parallel with COVID, East Africa, India, Pakistan and parts of the Middle East have been suffering unprecedented plagues of locusts, devouring everything in their path. Before COVID, there was a terrible virus called "Ebola" that spread across West Africa. It was like something out of a horror movie; people died through bleeding from the inside out. HIV AIDS has killed over forty million people.[11]

Other natural disasters are on the increase too. In my childhood, we hardly ever heard about earthquakes, tsunamis, flooding, bushfires or volcanic eruptions. In the last few years natural disasters are always in the news. The earthquake of 2010 in Haiti left 70% of the population in poverty. An earthquake in Japan in 2011 triggered a tsunami wave that was one hundred and thirty-three feet high and travelled six miles inland. It triggered a nuclear disaster at the Fukushima Daiichi power plant, and twenty thousand people died.

Typhoon Haiyan in 2013 was the strongest cyclone ever recorded and caused so much damage in the Philippines that four million people were displaced. In 2015 an Earthquake destroyed buildings across Nepal and killed nine thousand people in one afternoon. In 2017, Hurricane Harvey caused flooding at levels that scientists do not expect more than once every five hundred thousand years, and Hurricane Maria devasted Dominica and Puerto Rica, leaving millions without power for up to a year. In 2019, Cyclone Ida hit Southern Africa and killed one thousand three hundred people, while enormous wildfires destroyed vast areas of the Amazon and Indonesian rainforests.

UNICEF reported twenty-three natural disasters in 2023, causing fifty-seven point six billion dollars in damages. It is estimated that there were three times as many natural disasters in 2019 compared to 1980.[12]

Global warming is taking its toll on our environment.

And then there is war. Right now, the news is full of it. Russia invaded Ukraine in February 2022, and – at the time of writing – there seems to be no sign of peace. Israel and Hamas in Gaza are at full-scale war, but the actual conflict has been going on since 2006. Other places, including Sudan and South Sudan, Afghanistan, Ethiopia, Syria and Yemen, are all at war, but just not getting as much airtime in the news. Conflict is the number one cause of hunger in the world, and we have a global crisis with displaced people seeking refuge in other countries. The UN refugee agency reports one hundred and ten million forcibly displaced people worldwide in 2023.[13]

It is easy to feel depressed or scared when you look at statistics like this.

Yet, God tells us not to worry because these things are to be expected.

The disciples were asking Jesus about the end of the world and judgment day – in particular, when it would happen.

In Matthew Chapter 24, we can read Jesus' response. He first prophesies about the temple in Jerusalem, and this prophecy came true in 70 AD when the Romans destroyed Jerusalem:

"Jesus left the temple and was walking away when His disciples came up to Him to call His attention to its buildings. 'Do you see all these things?' He asked. 'Truly I tell you, not one stone here will be left on another; every one will be thrown down.' As Jesus was sitting on the Mount of Olives, the disciples came to Him privately. 'Tell us,' they said, 'When will this happen, and what will be the sign of Your coming and of the end of the age?' Jesus answered: 'Watch out that no one deceives you. For many will come in My name, claiming, 'I am the Messiah,' and will deceive many. You will hear of wars and rumours of wars but see to it that you are not alarmed. Such things must happen, but the end is still to come. Nation will rise against nation and kingdom against kingdom. There will be famines and earthquakes in various places. All these are the beginning of birth pains.'"

Can you see that we are living through what Jesus prophesied? There is a period of human history between Jesus' first and second coming, and these are called the end times because when He comes again, the world as we know it will end, and a new Heaven and Earth will be created. This is described in Revelation 21.

"Then I saw 'a new Heaven and a new earth,' for the first Heaven and the first earth had passed away, and there was no longer any sea. I saw the Holy City, the new Jerusalem, coming down out of Heaven from God, prepared as a bride beautifully dressed for her husband. And I heard a loud voice from the throne saying, 'Look! God's dwelling place is now among the people, and He will dwell with them. They will be His people, and God Himself will be with them and be their God. He will wipe every tear from their eyes. There will be no more death or mourning or crying or pain, for the old order of things has passed away'" (Revelation 21:1–4).

In the build-up to Jesus coming again, He says that we are to expect an increase in wars and natural disasters, which will worsen until the day He returns. That means we should expect another COVID-style pandemic and further wars and other disasters that are not yet in the news. I do not expect any political campaigns to get the better of global warming. Our planet is groaning under the destructive forces of humanity's greed, and it is going to take a supernatural intervention from God to put it right. He is the only one who can restore our planet, and the good news is that He has wonderfully promised to do so.

In the meantime, Jesus says not to worry. He refused to tell the disciples exactly when He would return. He simply said to watch out for the signs in the world and be prepared for the day of His coming. He warned that there would be increased hostility to Christians and that the love of many would grow cold. The organisation Open Doors reports that today, more than three hundred and sixty-five million people globally suffer high levels of persecution and discrimination for their faith.[14]

Jesus also warned that there would be an increase in false prophets trying to lead people astray. Some will claim to be the promised Messiah and may have what appears to be supernatural powers. We are warned not to be deceived by them. The return of Jesus the Messiah will be unmistakable because it will only happen after the ultimate natural (or should I say supernatural) disaster of the sun and stars ceasing to shine. No one on earth will be in any doubt about the return of the Son of God.

Many of us blame the world's problems on God, and a common objection I used to raise was to ask why a loving God would allow people to suffer. How can He let people starve or die of disease?

I see it so differently now. Mankind is the cause of suffering in the world. We have rejected God and His commands, and as a consequence, our world suffers and we all suffer with it. It is our greed that is destroying the planet, and it is man's politics and power hunger that causes war. If we loved our neighbour as ourselves, we would all be at peace. If we shared the resources that are plentiful on this earth, then there would be no poverty. Much disease is also caused by our own actions. Obesity drives cardiovascular disease and diabetes, smoking causes cancer, lack of access to clean water kills millions in the Third World. This is not God's plan for us, and the good news is that He has promised to put it all right by creating a new earth with no disease, death, war or famine.

So why doesn't God sort it out today rather than allow further suffering? The issue is that the solution is drastic. This perfect new world without suffering requires the removal of sin of any sort, so Judgement Day separates the wicked from the godly, the saved from the unsaved. I believe that Jesus is waiting until the last possible person in history has been saved from Hell before He returns. In the meantime, he tells us to wait and be prepared. How can we prepare? It's easy. We repent of our rejection of God and His ways and ask Jesus, the One who decides what happens to us, to be our Saviour.

I have also learned that the world has values that are the opposite of God's. For example, I was CEO of my own business, and the world sees me as wealthy and successful. Clare gave up her job as a buyer within Searle Pharmaceuticals to become a full-time mum when Amy was born. That was quite a sacrifice for her. The world sees motherhood as a lesser role than being in business and earning lots of money. God values the opposite. The fruit of my labour was money; the fruit of Clare's was our children. Their well-being, characters and beliefs have all been nurtured predominantly by Clare, and her always being there for them as a full-time mum has given them a strong sense of security. I will always be eternally thankful for all that she has done.

God values Clare's role over mine because she created a loving environment where her family could grow into the wonderful people they have become. Her sacrifice of a corporate role was worth it.

Our world seeks happiness but seeks it in the wrong ways because we value the wrong things.

Jesus spoke about this in His famous sermon on the Mount, which you can read in Matthew 5.

"He said, 'Blessed are the poor in spirit, for theirs is the kingdom of Heaven. Blessed are those who mourn, for they will be comforted. Blessed are the meek, for they will inherit the earth. Blessed are those who hunger and thirst for righteousness, for they will be filled. Blessed are the merciful, for they will be shown mercy. Blessed are the pure in heart, for they will see God. Blessed are the peacemakers, for they will be called children of God. Blessed are those who are persecuted because of righteousness, for theirs is the kingdom of Heaven. Blessed are you when people insult you, persecute you and falsely say all kinds of evil against you because of Me. Rejoice and be glad, because great is your reward in Heaven, for in the same way they persecuted the prophets who were before you" (Matthew 5:1–12).

Blessed means happy, and Jesus suggests that we will be happy for reasons that seem to be the opposite of what we chase in the world. We value strength and fighting for our rights. God values meekness and submission. That, by the way, does not mean that we are weak and pathetic. Actually, submitting to someone else is a real act of strength, particularly when you feel you are in the right. Jesus Himself submitted to the authorities who crucified Him when He had the power to stop it: an example of meekness and submission being a strength. An attitude of submission leads to peace in the home, at work and in our hearts. The problem is that we prefer to fight for our rights, and therefore, we lose peace.

The world values self-satisfaction, and we will go to any length to gain power, wealth, and enjoyment in the pursuit of happiness. God says that it is better to be in mourning than to be constantly striving after the things of the world. That is because the desires of the world are fleeting, and the goalposts are always moving. If you gain money or power, the initial thrill is quickly lost as you want more and fear losing what you have. Just look at the change in so many politicians from election night to a few months into their tenure.

Our world values fame and popularity, yet many become unhappy when they lose what they had or don't become as famous as they had hoped. Being liked is a very dangerous thing to base your happiness on because, one day, it will all disappear. Our children are suffering a crisis in mental health and self-worth because of this false doctrine of being popular and beautiful, promoted so aggressively through social media. God values us all just as we are. He has made us unique and loves us whether we are fat or thin, beautiful or ugly, black or white, male or female, rich or poor, academic or not, famous or not. True happiness comes when our identity comes from God and not from what the world demands.

People who seek their happiness in drugs, alcohol, gambling or sexual experiences soon find that what used to satisfy no longer works. They need more and more stimulus to feed their desire and plunge further into misery. God says you will be happy when you seek Him instead because He will give you lasting satisfaction and a deep sense of joy.

God values peacemakers – so needed in a world full of war and argument. When you read the vile content written on social media posts, you see the heart of humanity. We are rude and argumentative and like to tear people down. It must be horrible these days to be in the public eye. Instead, God wants us to build one another up and encourage.

I remember once, when Amy was a baby, we had a gas leak in the street. A man in a van came out at about 2 am and sat with music blaring out of his windows as he waited for a colleague to come and assist.

I was angry and got dressed to tell him to turn the noise down, as he was being selfish and inconsiderate. My angry words simply escalated the problem. A few minutes later, Clare came out with a cup of tea, some biscuits and a smile. He turned the music down, and the atmosphere changed immediately. Blessed are the peacemakers.

Our instincts when we are hurt are to retaliate and get revenge. God values forgiveness and turning the other cheek, and in this instance, when we choose to do what God commands, we avoid the fruit of bitterness in our lives. The only person who hurts when we do not forgive is ourselves.

The wonderful thing is that when we start to value what God values and turn away from chasing the empty desires of the world, we do find a deep-seated sense of peace and joy setting in. I believe that the world is becoming a more unhappy place because we are increasingly turning away from God, and therefore, our value system is upside down.

In the next chapter, I will summarise what I think are the main benefits of believing and trusting in Jesus.

Chapter 11
The Benefits of Being a Believer

"Praise the Lord, my soul, and forget not all His benefits –
who forgives all your sins and heals all your diseases,
who redeems your life from the pit and crowns you with
love and compassion, who satisfies your desires with
good things so that your youth is renewed like the
eagle's."

– Psalm 103:3–5

I can honestly say that I do not know how I could live my life without Jesus at the centre of it. He is there for me in the tough times and in the joyful times. I turn to Him for consolation when I am crying, upset, or worried, and likewise, when I am joyful, it is He whom I thank and praise.

There are so many benefits to being born again into a living relationship with Jesus Christ, some of which I have mentioned earlier.

Death

I am no longer afraid of death because I have a certainty as to where I am going. Heaven is real to me and, therefore, a great comfort. The person I am, will live on and be given a new, perfect body that will still be able to dance, sing, eat and talk with my friends. In a way, death is a release from a world full of darkness, and I will be going to a place of light, love and laughter.

There is definitely a difference between the funerals of believers and non-believers. Yes, we share the same sense of loss and grief, but the Christian funeral also has a sense of celebration. The sure hope of eternity and Heaven is a great comfort when we lose friends and family. My only fear is that some of those I love will not be there because they rejected Jesus as Saviour and chose not to accept His offer of eternity with Him.

Trusting God for Our Futures

I used to think that my future depended solely on me and my efforts. That attitude creates stress and sometimes disappointment. I failed my A-levels, so I beat myself up. I didn't get the job I wanted, so I felt that I was not good enough. That girl didn't want to go out with me, so I felt unattractive.

Replace that with an attitude that God is working out everything for my good and your whole outlook on life changes.

When I failed my A-levels, I had to take an extra year to do resits. In that year I made new friends for life. My best man at our wedding would not have been a friend if I had gone to university in a different year. God also uses hard knocks to teach us something; in this instance, I learnt about picking myself up, persevering and trying over and over again. That is a great character trait to have developed and has helped me in all sorts of trials.

God Has Helped Me Make Big Decisions in Life

There was a time at work when I was increasingly unhappy, and I was struggling with my boss. On a Sunday afternoon, the butterflies in my stomach would start, and I would enter work on a Monday morning, dreading going in. During this time, I applied for a job with a competitor.

The morning of the interview, I sat at my piano, singing worship songs and asking God for guidance. "Lord, is this the job for me? Give me a sign," I prayed. When it was time to drive to the interview, I shut the front door behind me and went to open the car. I had locked my keys in the house and couldn't get into the car. I then realised I had a door key hidden in a tree in the garden, so I retrieved it and tried to open the back door. It was bolted at the top, and I was stuck outside, unable to drive to the interview. I laughed aloud and said to the Lord, "OK, I get it, you don't want me to take this job. Thank you for the sign." At that point, the door swung open, and I was able to retrieve my keys.

I chose to drive to the interview because it was the right thing to do, despite knowing that God did not want me to take the job. They offered me the role and were surprised when I declined.

A few months later, the boss I was trying to escape from moved to the company that had offered me a role. She would have become my boss again if I had accepted the job. God saved me from making a bad decision.

By staying in my current role, I was given an expensive product that required the development of cost-effectiveness arguments to support its promotion. That gave me the skills that enabled me to work at Abacus and the eventual success that brought. God is interested in our long-term futures and sometimes, He chooses to close a door to us because it is the wrong option. I have learned that even when I am disappointed in the outcome of something, God's will is being worked out in my life. It is an attitude that brings peace and contentment.

Over and over again, I have seen that God prepares the way for our future. We have prayed for our daughters when they leave for university, and He has provided the right friends for them, the right courses and, eventually, the right jobs. I believe that God puts people in our lives for a purpose, including bringing Christians alongside us so that He can speak to those He is calling. It was no accident that God put Andy into my life in 1991 and then surrounded me with Christian neighbours. Now, I believe that He puts me into other people's lives for His purposes because I find it easy to share my faith. Sometimes, He has brought people into our lives so we can be family for them or support them financially.

When the girls left home, I mourned their departure, and yet when the Ukraine war started, we connected with Iryna, Andrii, and baby Matthew. We acted as hosts for them, and now they are family to us. God, in His goodness, saw a need in Clare and I and gave us another daughter with her family, not to replace our own girls but to add to those we love.

Hope in a Dark World

Hope is a powerful emotion, and it is linked to faith. My faith says that God is in control. Jesus says that He will return someday and restore the world to perfection. The more I trust God, the more I hope everything will turn out OK. To me, hope is more than wishful thinking like "I hope I get that job" or "I hope that my friend gets better." Hebrews 11 says that faith is confidence in what we hope for and assurance about what we do not see. I don't hope that there is life after death; I know it for certain, and that fills me with a feeling called hope. It's the opposite of despair. So when I look at the news and see disease and war and suffering, I choose not to despair. My faith lets me hope for a better future that will come when Jesus returns.

Wisdom

I don't always get a big sign regarding a decision, but I do know that when I pray, God provides wisdom. He is all-knowing and all-wise, and His Spirit lives in us when we ask Jesus into our lives. The Holy Spirit speaks to us and helps us make good decisions when we listen to Him.

I have had to sack people in my role as a boss, and it was the one aspect that I would find most difficult because I care about people and their livelihoods. However, in business, there are times when someone is in the wrong job, and it is impacting on themselves and on others. I would often wrestle for weeks and months over big HR decisions like this and through prayer, if I got to a place of peace in my heart, then I could go through with the termination process.

I do believe that in those dark days at Abacus when I was thrown into the deep end of running a business, the Lord gave me the ability to make all sorts of decisions about legal and accounting issues, staffing, customers, marketing and communications. Wisdom is a spiritual gift, and it is sensible to ask God for it. In my life post-Abacus, I have found that several business owners have asked me to act as an advisor, and I get a lot of people seeking counsel through my personal life. Most of these people are not Christians, but I think they recognise the wisdom that I know comes from God.

I believe in the spiritual discipline of fasting and prayer. The idea is not to eat and instead spend time in prayer and reading the Bible. So often, these are the times when I will get an answer to something I am wrestling with, and I can make a decision with peace in my heart.

Identity

The world is suffering an identity crisis, and it is creating terrible misery for so many, particularly the youngest generation, who have grown up with the pressure of social media. God has made us uniquely different: male and female, black and white, large and small. Instead of celebrating who God has made each of us to be, far too many of us are trying to choose our own identity and are striving to become what we think the world sees as perfect. We then become unhappy deep within ourselves when we cannot be these ideals.

When I was seventeen, I realised I had started to go bald. It really affected me and my confidence. At work, I would feel good if sales were up and bad if sales were down. I would be happy after a promotion or salary increase until I realised I wanted more a while later. When your identity is based upon an ideal that you cannot quite reach, then you are destined to be constantly dissatisfied and unhappy.

My identity is now as an adopted son of the King of Kings. I am a precious child of God, chosen by Him at the beginning of time. I don't have to worry about my looks, cleverness, achievements, popularity or relationships in order to be happy and fulfilled. I don't need to strive to be something or someone else. I am me, warts and all, and it is hugely releasing when you accept yourself for who you are, knowing that God loves you today and always, and that will never change.

I have friends who seek to please earthly fathers who have never expressed that they are proud of them. They spend their lives trying to achieve and do things that will gain the approval of their dad. The wonderful thing about our Father in Heaven is that we don't need to achieve, perform, or be perfectly good for His approval. He loves us for who we are and longs to be in our lives.

Anxiety Replaced by Peace

There is a wonderful sense of joy and peace that comes supernaturally when you pray and then trust God for the outcome. I am a natural worrier, and that tendency is still in me. However, I have learned over the years that when I pray, my worries are replaced by His peace.

2023 was a challenging year. We left our church family after eighteen years, feeling hurt and frustrated for various reasons. At Christmas, my mum had a fall and broke her hip. She was blind and suffering from dementia, so we had to make the difficult decision to put her into a care home. I then got gallstones and had to have emergency surgery to remove my gallbladder as I also had pancreatitis. At the same time, Clare's mum, who was ninety, had a fall, and she, too, had to go into a care home. Clare was diagnosed with diabetes.

Life happens, and sometimes, when many things occur simultaneously, it is difficult to cope. That is when my faith makes all the difference.

In June 2023, I had a two-day retreat and business meeting with International Health Partners, a Christian charity that ships donated medicines to the Third World and into areas of crisis. I am a Trustee and had this meeting in my diary from the previous year. We were staying at Waverley Abbey which has been a place of continuous prayer for over a thousand years. I believe you can sense God's closeness in this place in a very tangible way. A real sense of peace flows from it, being a historic place of so much prayer.

On the Saturday morning, I decided to go for an early morning walk before breakfast and as I left the hotel area, I heard the sound of running water. There was a weir across the road with gushing torrents of water on one side and an absolutely still mill pond on the other. Immediately, I got a sense that my life in 2023 had been like that rushing, tumultuous water and a picture that God was the weir and on the other side was peace and stillness. The words of Psalm 23 came into my mind as I walked along the river through lovely fields to the ruins of the Abbey.

- The Lord is my Shepherd, I lack nothing. I found myself weeping as I felt God remind me of all the good things in my life. He really has blessed me abundantly, and truly, I can say that I lack nothing. He is my Shepherd, guiding, protecting and providing.

- He makes me lie down in green pastures and leads me beside still waters. As I meditated on these words, I pondered how God can make us lie down, and I then realised that God had placed me at Waverley Abbey for a purpose. He had chosen this particular weekend after a really tough year, and I had literally walked along a beautiful river that was so still in the early morning light. I was watching herons and other wildlife and just enjoying the beauty of His creation. I had literally sat down in the green pastures of the ruined Abbey.

- He restores my soul. That is why I was there at that moment. God, the Holy Spirit, washed over me. I didn't even try to pray. He was spiritually ministering to me. He washed away the hurts from church, the sadness of placing our mothers into care homes and the worry of personal physical ill health. I can honestly say that I was utterly filled with the love and peace of God, and all the negative experiences and emotions of the prior year were just dealt with;

a fantastic feeling, and that peace has stayed with me.

Miraculous Intervention

In the Bible, we read of the many miracles of Jesus: Raising people from death, healing them and driving out demons were just some examples. He still does that today through the power of His Holy Spirit. Before He ascended to Heaven, He told his disciples that He would send them a Helper to do His work on earth. That happened at Pentecost, and Jesus' disciples, filled with the Holy Spirit, have been praying for miracles in His name ever since. Anyone who asks Jesus into their life becomes His disciple and becomes filled with His Holy Spirit. We all, therefore, have the power to ask for healing in His name.

When Izzy was about three, Clare took her to the opticians for a routine check-up. She came home with a letter for a referral to a doctor. We opened the letter and saw that the optician was worried that she had a retinal blastoma. He had drawn a diagram to explain what he had seen. I googled "retinal blastoma" and found that it typically affected children of her age, and it was a cancer that could spread from the retina to the brain. It might mean the removal of her eye and possibly lead to death. We were terrified and had a sleepless night. The following morning was a Sunday, so we went to church. The elders laid hands on Izzy during the service, and the whole church prayed for healing. They also prayed that we would get speedy access to the medical professionals so that we wouldn't have this hanging over us for weeks.

After the service, Clare said, "I know that she has been healed." I have to confess that my faith was not that strong, and so I remained anxious.

The following day, we rang the GP first thing, and he got us an appointment with an eye specialist at the hospital. We were there by 10 am, and a Registrar put drops in Izzy's eyes to look for what the optician had seen. She seemed to be taking forever, and my heart was in my mouth, waiting to hear what the doctor said. At that moment, the chorus of a song we sang at church came into my mind. "I will trust, I will trust, I will trust in You." Over and over again, these words went round and round. God was telling me to trust Him.

Eventually, the Registrar told us that she wanted to get a second opinion from her Consultant, and so we went into another office for further investigations. After what seemed forever, I blurted out, "Please tell us, what have you found?" The doctor replied, "The issue is that we cannot find anything wrong, and we don't understand what the optician saw. Maybe there was a speck of dust on their equipment." The relief was enormous, and in that moment, I knew what had happened. I told the doctor that the only thing that happened between Friday and Monday was prayer and the laying on of hands on the Sunday. I do believe that God provided a miracle and we left the hospital praising Him.

It was not the first time, either. Clare's sister had been diagnosed with some kind of ovarian cyst and had an operation booked for the following morning. We drove to her house to pray for healing in Jesus' name. It was one of the most powerful sensations of prayer I have ever experienced. I felt the presence of God at work, and my fingers tingled as we prayed. Andrea was swaying, and something enormous was going on. The following day, when the doctors went in with the laparoscope, all they found was scar tissue and no cyst. Again, we know that she was healed through prayer.

In Eswatini, I have a friend who was on death's door with the HIV Aids that she had contracted from her husband. Another pastor friend prayed over her, and she said that she felt like she was having a blood transfusion, so she decided to get a blood test. When she returned for the results, the doctor said as she entered his office, "Ah, my miracle lady." Her CD4 count, the marker for HIV infection, had returned to normal – simply through prayer.

Of course, there are other times when we have prayed for people, and they have not improved. I cannot answer why sometimes God chooses to heal and sometimes He does not, but we will always pray for healing and trust Him for the outcome.

God Makes Me a Better Version of Myself

I spoke about this in an earlier chapter. The Holy Spirit makes us sensitive to our wrongdoings and prompts us to confess. He shows us the areas of our characters that need refining, and bit by bit, over the years, He softens us and moulds us into the people He wants us to be: more loving, more gentle and kind, more self-controlled and less angry, more patient and tolerant, more generous, less proud and self-seeking. I am still a work in progress but certainly a different person to the one I used to be because of His prompting and occasional rebukes.

There are so many other ways that God blesses that I don't have space for it all. He is the glue in our marriage and the peace in our home. He has answered so many prayers over the years, and I am sure that He blesses in ways unseen. There will be things in my life that didn't happen because God intervened. I am just so glad that He is there and will be there one day when I cross over from death into eternal life.

SIMON HOWARD

SIMON HOWARD

142

Chapter 12
Some Promises of God

In this final chapter, I simply invite you to read some of the many promises that God makes in the Bible. It really is a book full of good news and is the antidote to all the bad news we hear in our papers and on our TVs.

1. He will make your path straight.

"Trust in the Lord with all your heart, and do not lean on your own understanding. In all your ways acknowledge Him, and He will make straight your paths." – Proverbs 3:5–6

As an atheist, I was leaning on my own limited understanding. Now, as a Christian, I feel like God has opened my eyes and given me a glimpse of His much better perspective on the world as we know it. God really does lead us on the right path of life, and the only thing we have to do is submit to Him and then trust. This is especially important when life seems difficult. I might wonder why I am on this particular path that is painful but I am always comforted when I acknowledge that God knows what He is doing and why I am in this place.

2. God gives wisdom to those who ask.

"If any of you lacks wisdom, let him ask God, who gives generously to all without reproach, and it will be given him." – James 1:5

When I was a new Christian, my church ran some teaching sessions on spiritual gifts, and we each had a chance to pray for some aspects of God's giftings. I asked for wisdom, just like King Solomon did. I believe that God gives a supernatural ability to know how to make the right decision and I am sure that this contributed to the success of my business. More importantly, He gives us the wisdom to understand the deep spiritual truths He speaks of in the Bible.

Are you thinking about moving house or job? Do you have financial or relationship problems? Are you studying for exams or doing something daunting for the first time? Are you out of your comfort zone as a parent or not sure what to do with your life? Then, ask Jesus what to do and wait for the solution to settle in your heart and mind.

3. Call on Him and He will answer.

"Call upon Me in the day of trouble; I will deliver you, and you shall glorify Me." – Psalm 50:15

We all have difficult times in life. I am so glad that I worship a God who listens and answers when I pray. Please note that prayer does not always result in what you expect. An answer can be "yes", "no" or "wait". My challenge has always been wanting the answer to my prayer immediately, and I have had to learn that sometimes God closes a door or teaches me patience through faithfully waiting in prayer, sometimes for years.

4. Believe you have received what you have asked for in prayer.

"Therefore I tell you, whatever you ask in prayer, believe that you have received it, and it will be yours." – Mark 11:24

This can be a challenge. When we pray, do we believe that God has heard and has answered? Faith requires us to trust that God has heard and that He is answering our prayer, even if it does not yet seem obvious.

5. He gives strength to the weary.

"But those who hope in the Lord will renew their strength. They will soar on wings like eagles; they will run and not grow weary, they will walk and not be faint." – Isaiah 40:31

This was the scripture that a lady shared with me when we visited a church in Torquay a few weeks after Andy had been killed. God reminded me that He was giving me the strength to run Abacus during that time of crisis. Note that for our strength to be renewed, we have to hope in the Lord, so if you are weary, you first have to put your hope in Jesus.

6. He will give you rest.

"Come to Me, all who labour and are heavy laden, and I will give you rest. Take My yoke upon you, and learn from Me, for I am gentle and lowly in heart, and you will find rest for your souls. For My yoke is easy, and My burden is light." – Matthew 11:28–30

This scripture hangs in a framed picture on my dressing room wall. God spoke to me through it when I was heavy burdened at work and really in need of emotional rest. I realised I wanted to wear His yoke, not the one of my business, and it resulted in me deciding to sell Abacus in order to directly serve God in other ways.

So many of us need to find rest for our souls, and I have experienced that abundantly in my thirty-year relationship with Jesus.

7. He will meet all your needs.

"And my God will supply every need of yours according to his riches in glory in Christ Jesus." – Philippians 4:19

There is a difference between needs and wants. If you spent all your time praying to win the lottery or to be famous or to fulfil some other worldly desire, I do not believe that God will answer, because your motives are wrong. But we all have basic needs of love, food and security, and I do believe that God promises to provide these.

8. He will give you the desires of your heart.

"Delight yourself in the Lord, and He will give you the desires of your heart." – Psalm 37:4

This is similar to the verse above and requires us to desire the right things. Note that we have to first delight in the Lord. When we seek Him and when we are filled with the Holy Spirit, then our heart's desires are shaped by Him. I didn't set out to run a business or to get rich. That was not my heart's desire; it just happened. My driving force is to be in the right place with God. I desire to please Him; I want to be the person He wants me to be. I want to have my heart broken for the things that break His.

9. All things will be provided when you seek first His kingdom.

"Seek first the Kingdom of God and His righteousness, and all these things will be added to you." – Matthew 6:31–33

This is another scripture that reminds us of our prayer priorities. We should seek a relationship with God before anything else because when we have restored that broken relationship with Him, everything will be provided. When you look at the structure of the Lord's prayer, only one line ("Give us our daily bread") is about providing for needs. The rest is about praising our Father in Heaven, confessing our sins because these keep us from hearing from Him and giving thanks for what He has already provided.

It is surprising how many of our prayers are about asking God for things. Can you imagine how you would feel as a parent if the only time your child ever spoke to you was to ask for something? Sometimes, it is just good to quietly spend time with God, thanking Him for the good things in your life or simply because you have just seen a beautiful sunset or rainbow.

We tried to use the teaspoon (tsp) prayer structure with our kids when they were little.

Thank you

Sorry

Please

Despite its simplicity, it remains an excellent way to develop your relationship with God. Our prayer life should be open and honest and we should feel comfortable crying out to Him in despair and asking Him questions like "Why is this happening?" or "What should I do?" Seek God through your prayer life. Don't just ask Him for things.

10. His love never fails.

"For the mountains may depart and the hills be removed, but My steadfast love shall not depart from you." – Isaiah 54:10

Love is a basic need of all humans, and there is only one love that can be guaranteed, and that is God's. Nothing you have done in your past will stop Him from loving you. His greatest desire is for you to turn to Him and receive His love for you. There is a famous Bible story called "The Prodigal Son" about a lad who took his father's inheritance and travelled the world squandering it in wild living. I would rename the story "The Parable of the Loving Father." Day after day for many years, this father sadly looks down the road, hoping for his son to return home. One glorious day, he sees what he has been waiting for and joyfully runs to hug the missing son who has returned. That is what God is doing for each one of us. He is longing for you and me to come home to Him so He can throw a party and lavish His love upon us.

11. The Lord will fight for you.

"Fear not, stand firm, and see the salvation of the Lord, which He will work for you today. For the Egyptians whom you see today, you shall never see again. The Lord will fight for you, and you have only to be silent." – Exodus 14:13–14

This is a fantastic promise. When I was young, there was a bully on my street who I was scared of. He challenged me to a fight, which I declined. He threatened to set his dad on me, and I remember saying that my dad had Judo belts and would fight his dad on my behalf. There is something comforting when you think of your dad as strong and able to fight your corner for you. Imagine how it makes us feel when we realise that we have the King of the universe on our side, helping us through the battles of life. There is nothing He cannot do for us, including saving us from death, so what is there to fear?

12. He will never forsake you.

"Be strong and courageous. Do not fear or be in dread of them, for it is the Lord your God who goes with you. He will not leave you or forsake you." – Deuteronomy 31:6

I love the idea that God will never leave us. Husbands and wives sometimes split up, children sometimes fall out with their parents, and friends sometimes lose touch. Our faithful God will always be there for us, and Jesus will be waiting for us when we cross over from death into life.

13. All things work for good for those who love God.

"And we know that for those who love God all things work together for good, for those who are called according to His purpose." – Romans 8:28

Sometimes, life brings its knocks. This promise brings hope during tough times. When I don't get that job, it is because God has got something else lined up for me. When that offer on the house we want falls through, it is because God wants us to live somewhere else. I shared earlier that I got stuck in a negative equity trap for years on my first house. I couldn't see it then, but God used that experience for my good. He used financial hardship to make me less material-minded and more dependent upon Him. A good prayer to pray during hard times is to ask, "What are You doing through this, Lord?" Often, you will find out, but at a later stage.

14. He will exalt the humble.

"Whoever exalts himself will be humbled, and whoever humbles himself will be exalted." – Matthew 23:12

Sometimes, the world looks unfair. Some people seem to grab all the power and money and get away with wicked behaviour, whilst others suffer in terrible conditions. It frustrates me when I visit Africa regularly because the continent has all the resources it needs. There should be no poverty. Unfortunately, far too many political leaders abuse their power and syphon off the wealth for themselves. Even charitable aid does not always go to the cause that it was intended for.

This promise from God makes me feel better. One day, God will judge all people and those who were humbled in this life will be exalted or raised up. The abusers will be humbled. Interestingly, the scripture talks about those who humble themselves will be raised up. I think we humble ourselves when we get on our knees and put God first and then sacrificially put others' needs before our own.

15. He forgives us when we forgive others.

"Forgive, and you will be forgiven." – Luke 6:37

Forgiveness is an act of love, and we should do it even if the other party does not apologise. The result of forgiving is that it frees us from bitterness and is amazingly liberating. I once heard a radio phone-in for the parents of children who had been murdered. One lady called in, and her son had been murdered twenty years before. She was still bitter and wanted revenge on the murderer. A Christian lady rang in, and her child had more recently been killed. She stated that she had chosen to forgive the murderer, and you could hear the difference in tone and emotions between the two callers. Of course, both would always grieve the loss of their child, but one was going to be freed from the harmful impact of bitterness.

Interestingly, scripture seems to link forgiveness and being forgiven by God. The Lord's Prayer states it nicely: "Forgive us our sins as we forgive those who sin against us." God calls us to forgive one another because He knows the harmful effects of not doing so.

16. He forgives us when we confess our sins.

"If we confess our sins, He is faithful and just to forgive us our sins and to cleanse us from all unrighteousness." – 1 John 1:9

A related promise is that Jesus will forgive all of us, whatever we have done and however bad we have been. His death on the cross was enough to pay any penalty for any crime we have committed, His punishment in our place dealt with it all. The only part we have to play is to turn to Him and repent, to say sorry, and then He promises to make us clean from all our wrongdoings. This is the process that makes us fit for Heaven.

17. He has redeemed you.

"He has delivered us from the domain of darkness and transferred us to the kingdom of His beloved Son, in whom we have redemption, the forgiveness of sins." – Colossians 1:13–14

This promise sounds a bit theologically complicated. It means that Jesus has paid the price for a lifetime of our sins. Jesus redeemed the thief on the cross next to Him. He recognised Jesus for who He was and said, "Remember me when You come into Your Kingdom." That simple request was enough for Jesus to respond, "Today you will be with Me in paradise." When we turn to Him, Jesus takes us from a Kingdom of darkness into one of light.

18. He has given us eternal life.

"For God so loved the world, that He gave His only Son, that whoever believes in Him should not perish but have eternal life." – John 3:16

This is possibly the most famous scripture in the New Testament, and what a promise it is. We are given eternal life through Jesus. Therefore, we no longer need to fear death or worry about whether we have been deserving enough for Heaven. Jesus has unlocked the door and welcomes us in; all we have to do is believe in Him.

19. He has adopted you.

"He predestined us for adoption to Himself as sons through Jesus Christ, according to the purpose of His will." – Ephesians 1:5

I find this amazing. We are told that when we become believers, we are literally adopted into God's family. We become His sons and daughters, which means that we are brothers and sisters to one another. As a son, I have an inheritance that God promises, one that will never rust or decay because it is stored up for me in Heaven and will last into eternity.

20. He will never blot your name from the Book of Life.

"The one who conquers will be clothed thus in white garments, and I will never blot his name out of the Book of Life. I will confess his name before my Father and before His angels." – Revelation 3:5

What a wonderful promise! By Christ's blood, we cannot lose our place in His kingdom. Trouble may come, but if you have received the free gift of eternal life, it cannot ever be stolen from you. I still think and do wrong things. People irritate me, and I get angry. I can say sharp things to those I love. You wouldn't want to hear what is going on in my thoughts sometimes. However, despite all of that, my place in God's Kingdom remains assured, all because of Jesus.

21. The devil will flee from you if you resist.

"Submit yourselves therefore to God. Resist the devil, and he will flee from you." – James 4:7

I said earlier that I believe that Satan is real because Jesus spoke a lot about him. His influence is at work in the world, and he is spiritually powerful. He is a tempter and deceiver. He causes division and strife and is determined to try to break our relationship with God and one another. Thankfully, Jesus is more powerful, and we are told that the devil will flee when we command him to do so in Jesus' name. The Bible tells us that God gives us spiritual armour when we pray, and that armour protects our minds and our hearts. If you have dark thoughts, pray in Jesus' name for those thoughts to go. If Satan is telling you that you are worthless, then ask Jesus to show you how He sees you. If you are addicted to something, ask Jesus to break those addictions.

22. He will set you free.

"So if the Son sets you free, you will be free indeed." – John 8:36

I used to think that religion was all about a whole load of rules that would spoil fun: "Do not do this, and do not do that." God does call us to avoid certain things and do others, but for our own good. Religions can indeed be restrictive, telling you how you should dress and making you feel bad when you do something wrong. That is not what Jesus came to do. He really does emotionally set us free from the things that bind us. My charity helps to fund two rehabilitation centres for addicts. The programme consists of a twelve-month residential course for men and women, many of whom also have trauma and mental health issues. When you meet these people and hear of the change that Jesus has brought into their lives, you cannot deny the power of the Holy Spirit at work in them. Jesus truly releases people from the things that bind them.

23. Your old self is dead.

"We know that our old self was crucified with Him in order that the body of sin might be brought to nothing, so that we would no longer be enslaved to sin." – Romans 6:6

The Bible tells us that when we ask Jesus into our lives, our old self dies, and we are born again. That is what the process of baptism celebrates. Our old self dies (represented by going under the water) and when we reemerge from the water, this represents our new selves rising again into a new life free from the things that once bound us.

24. He has prepared us a place.

"My Father's house has many rooms; if that were not so, would I have told you that I am going there to prepare a place for you? And if I go and prepare a place for you, I will come back and take you to be with Me that you also may be where I am. You know the way to the place where I am going." – John 14:2–4

Jesus taught so much about Heaven, or, as He called it often, the Kingdom of God. That is what He came to do. To prepare a way for us to get there and live with Him for eternity. This is so personal. He has prepared an individual room for you and me to go to and He will come back and take us to that room He has prepared. It's like a dad creating a nursery for his unborn child and then excitedly bringing the baby home after it has been born.

25. He is coming again soon.

"Behold, I am coming soon, bringing My recompense with Me, to repay each one for what he has done." – Revelation 22:12

We spoke earlier about biblical prophecy. So much of it has already come true, and Jesus fulfilled all of the prophecies about the coming of the Messiah. The only currently unfulfilled ones are about the Messiah's second coming and judgement day. Jesus warned us of the increase in wars and environmental problems that will happen in the run-up to that day. One key event was that the nation of Israel would be reformed after the Jews had been scattered over the earth. That happened in 1948 after World War Two. Jesus told us of the signs leading up to Armageddon and commanded us not to be afraid. Instead, we are to be prepared for the day of His return.

So let me ask you a question. Are you ready for Judgement Day? Are you ready to meet your Maker and to give an account for the life you have lived?

Conclusion

"Ask and it will be given to you; seek and you will find; knock and the door will be opened to you."

– Matthew 7:7

I wrote this book because I want you to know that God is real. I want you to know that He can make a massive difference in your life now and that He offers you life after death. He offers hope and brings peace into a world full of fear and division. Jesus said that He is the light of the world and whoever follows Him will never walk in darkness but will have the light of life (John 8:12). I discovered the truth of this when I turned from atheism to trusting in Him. At the point that I said sorry for rejecting Him and asking Jesus into my life, the Holy Spirit filled me powerfully. It was real, both physically and emotionally, and I have felt the power of God at work in my heart and in my mind ever since.

I hope you have seen that faith does not require you to put aside common sense and logic. In fact, I hope that you see that the evidence for God is overwhelming. Over thirty years as a Christian, my personal experiences of God have been so powerful that I am left with no doubts whatsoever. I know where I will go when I die and when I am anxious, He is the first person I turn to for help. It is so much easier to get through the ups and downs of life when you are trusting in an Almighty God who knows everything, sees everything and can fix anything for those who put their trust in Him.

So, let me close with a challenge. The scripture at the head of this chapter says that if you seek, you will find. God will become real to you, just like He did with me if you truly seek Him. Will you go beyond closing the last page of this book and investigate further? I invite you to.

My atheistic views were based on ignorance as I had never read the Bible, prayed, gone to church or spoken with anyone about faith. I found God when I started looking and asking the right questions to the right people. This seeking is not just an intellectual exercise. That is the mistake that many people make, and one I also made for too long. God is not an idea that you either believe or not. He is a person with whom you can have a relationship. His Spirit can communicate with our spirit and, consequently, change how we are feeling and what we are thinking.

My personal experiences with God started when I dealt with the sin in my life and submitted to Jesus as Lord. You will meet Him through prayer and in singing praises to Him. You will meet Him when you read the Bible and talk about Him with others who are a bit further down the faith journey than you are.

Imagine if you were going to invest all your savings on the stock market to create a pension pot to live on for the rest of your life. I hope you would meet with expert advisors and discuss all the options. I hope that you would research in great detail your investment decision because if you got it wrong, the consequences could be catastrophic.

You would probably be even more diligent in assessing the risks if you were about to do something that could mean life or death, such as the safety of the parachute harness you had just put on or the effectiveness of the latest cancer drug you are about to take.

Well, I would like this book's key take-home message to be that we all have a decision to make about Jesus and whether He is who He claimed to be. Is He really the Way, the Truth and the Life? Is He really the only way to the Father? The only way to Heaven? If this is true, then you risk an eternity in Hell by rejecting Him. Surely, that deserves further investigation as it will be much better to meet Jesus the Shepherd than Jesus the Judge when you die.

I recommend that you join a local Alpha course, where you can have a meal and watch some videos that trigger discussion with people who have a range of opinions and experiences.

Try reading the Bible, maybe starting with the Gospels (Matthew, Mark, Luke or John). Many phone-based apps will give you a daily reading and a commentary from an expert. You will be amazed at how often God will say something relevant to you through tools like these.

Above all, pray and ask God to reveal Himself to you.

My ultimate desire is for you to ask Jesus into your life and gain the riches of a life with Him. If you are ready to take this step, you could consider praying something like this:

Lord Jesus, I accept that I cannot understand everything, but I acknowledge that I have rejected You all my life. I have said, done and thought wrong things, and I ask You to forgive me. I repent of my past and ask You, Jesus, to be my Lord and Saviour. I believe that You died on a cross and came to life again. I believe that You have paid the penalty for my sins, and I ask that You wash me clean. Come, Lord Jesus, and make me new. Fill me, Holy Spirit, so that I may know that You are real and in my life.

Amen.

"The Lord bless you and keep you; the Lord make His face shine on you and be gracious to you; the Lord turn His face toward you and give you peace"
(Numbers 6:24–26).

About the Author

Simon studied microbiology and worked in the pharmaceutical industry before running Abacus, a business he sold in 2012.

He is now a trustee for various charities and mentors business owners, helping them to grow their companies.

He is married to Clare and they have three daughters: Amy, Isabelle and Eliza.

Appendix
Prophecies About the Messiah that Jesus Fulfilled

1. Born of a Virgin

   - Prophecy: Isaiah 7:14 foretold that a virgin would conceive and bear a son.

   - Fulfilment: Jesus was born of the Virgin Mary (Matthew 1:22–23).

2. From the Lineage of Abraham, Jesse, Jacob, David and the Tribe of Judah

   - Prophecy: Genesis 22:18, Isaiah 11, Numbers 24:17, Genesis 49:10, Jeremiah 23:5–6.

   - Fulfilment: Matthew 1 and Luke 3:33.

3. Born in Bethlehem

   - Prophecy: Micah 5:2 predicted that the Messiah would be born in Bethlehem.

   - Fulfilment: Jesus was born in Bethlehem (Luke 2:4–7).

4. He Would Spend His Childhood in Egypt

   - Prophecy: Hosea 11:1

   - Fulfilment: Matthew 2:13–15

5. His Coming Would be Foretold by a Messenger

   - Prophecy: Isaiah 40:3

   - Fulfilment: Matthew 3; John the Baptist.

6. Rejected by His Own People

   - Prophecy: Isaiah 53:3 anticipated that the Messiah would be despised and rejected. Also read Psalm 118:22–23.

   - Fulfilment: Jesus faced rejection and hostility (John 1:11).

7. Riding into Jerusalem on a Donkey

   - Prophecy: Zechariah 9:9 described the Messiah's entry into Jerusalem.

   - Fulfilment: Jesus rode a donkey into Jerusalem (Matthew 21:1–11).

8. Silent Before Accusers

   - Prophecy: Isaiah 53:7 predicted that the Messiah would remain silent during His trial.

   - Fulfilment: Jesus did not defend Himself before Pilate (Matthew 27:12–14)

9. Betrayal for 30 Pieces of Silver

   - Prophecy: Zechariah 11:12–13 spoke of the Messiah being betrayed for a price. Psalm 41:9 shows betrayal by a friend who shared bread.

   - Fulfilment: Judas betrayed Jesus for 30 pieces of silver (Matthew 26:14–16).

10. Pierced Hands and Feet

- Prophecy: Psalm 22:16 describes the piercing of the Messiah's hands and feet.
- Fulfilment: Jesus' crucifixion involved nails through His hands and feet (John 20:25–27).

11. Suffering and Death

- Prophecy: Isaiah 53 describes the suffering and sacrificial death of the Messiah.
- Fulfilment: Jesus' crucifixion fulfilled this prophecy (Matthew 27:32–56).
- "He was assigned a grave with the wicked and with the rich in His death though He had done no violence..." Hanging alongside Him were two thieves and when He died He was put into the grave allotted to Joseph of Arimathea, a wealthy man.

12. His Bones Would Not Be Broken

- Prophecy: Numbers 9:12 ("Passover Lamb"); Psalm 34:20.
- Fulfilment: John 19:31–33.

13. Resurrection

- Prophecy: Psalm 16:10 foretold that the Messiah would not see decay.
- Fulfilment: Jesus rose from the dead on the third day (Acts 2:31).

14. Discuss: What do we think about what is going on in the world today? For example, COVID, starvation, environmental warming, earthquakes, tornadoes, bushfires, volcanoes, wars (Ukraine/Russia; Israel/Gaza; Sudan, Yemen, Afghanistan, Ethiopia, Syria).

15. Read Matthew 24: A prophecy that Jesus spoke.

16. Pray for the world.

References

Richardson. How Many Bibles Are Sold Each Year in the World.' *Richardson's Books*. (2023): https://richardsonsbooks.com/how-many-bibles-are-sold-each-year-in-the-world-evaluated-by-experts/

[2] Famous Scientists. '34 Great Scientists Who Were Committed Christians.' *Famous Scientists: The Art of Genius*. Available at: https://www.famousscientists.org/great-scientists-christians/

[3] Hummel, C. E. 'The Faith Behind the Famous: Isaac Newton.' *Christian History Institute*. Available at: https://christianhistoryinstitute.org/magazine/article/faith-behind-the-famous-isaac-newton

[4] Dickson, J. Is Jesus History? (The Good Book Company, 2019)

[5] Wallace, J. 'The Old Testament is Filled with Fulfilled Prophecy.' *Bible Study Tools*. (2016): https://www.biblestudytools.com/bible-study/topical-studies/the-old-testament-is-filled-with-fulfilled-prophecy-11652232.html

[6] Kiprop, V. 'Are There More Grains of Sand on Earth or Stars in the Universe?' *WorldAtlas*. (2018): https://www.worldatlas.com/articles/are-there-more-grains-of-sand-or-stars-in-the-earth.html

7   Kiprop, V. 2018. 'Are There More Grains of Sand on Earth or Stars in the Universe?' *WorldAtlas*. (2018): https://www.worldatlas.com/articles/are-there-more-grains-of-sand-or-stars-in-the-earth.html

8 Kindersley, D. History Year by Year: The Ultimate Visual Guide to Events that Shaped the World. (Penguin Random House, 2024), p. 24.

9 Lewis, C.S. Mere Christianity (Touchstone Books, 1996).

10 World Population by Country 2024. Available at: https://worldpopulationreview.com/

1 Kluger, J. TIME. 'A New Report Shows the True COVID-19 Death Toll May Be Three Times Higher Than We Thought', 4 February 2021 in Taboola Feed [online database]. Available at: https://time.com/6156774/covid-19-deaths-worldwide-estimate/

12 WHO. HIV and AIDS. *World Health Organisation*. (2023): https://www.who.int/news-room/fact-sheets/detail/hiv-aids

13 Buchholz, K. Statista. 'Natural Disasters on the Rise Around the Globe', 25 August 2020 in Statista Content and Design [online database]. Available at: https://www.statista.com/chart/22686/number-of-natural-disasters-globally/

14 UNHCR. 2024. Refugee Data Finder. *The UN Refugee Agency*. (2024): https://www.unhcr.org/refugee-statistics/

15 Open Doors. World Watch List. (2023): https://www.opendoors.org/en-US/persecution/countries/

About PublishU

PublishU is transforming the world of publishing.

PublishU has developed a new and unique approach to publishing books, offering a three-step guided journey to becoming a globally published author!

We enable hundreds of people a year to write their book within 100-days, publish their book in 100-days and launch their book over 100-days to impact tens of thousands of people worldwide.

The journey is transformative, one author said,

"I never thought I would be able to write a book, let alone in 100 days... now I'm asking myself what else have I told myself that can't be done that actually can?'"

To find out more visit
www.PublishU.com

Printed in Great Britain
by Amazon